When Life Becomes
A Love Story

Sonia Matthews

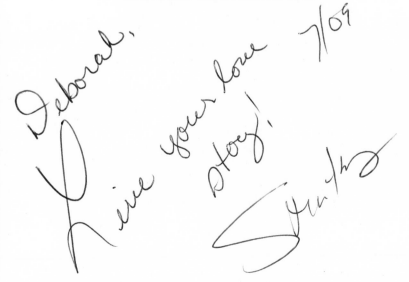

Published by Amadi Publishing, LLC 2008
5810 Kingstowne Center Dr.
Suite 120-234
Kingstowne, VA 22315

Printed in the United States of America

ISBN-13: 978-0-9815874-0-0
ISBN-10: 0-9815874-0-2

AMADI PUBLISHING

www.soniamatthews.com

Thank you...

... Persia, my awesome editor, for talking to me from your heart; for being patient and honest and taking my story and transforming it into a great one. You truly have a gift.

... Sue Anne, my other awesome editor, for taking one last look and being good at what you do;

... George, for creating such a beautiful cover and not asking me for any money. Check's in the mail;

... Aisha, for lending me that beautiful face for my cover;

... Neil, my friend forever, for planting the seed.

... S. Jones, for contributing Made Whole Again, I live In My Dreams, Co-authoring Your Man Took Me and Committed;

... Jill, for continuing to encourage me;

... Monica, for being brutally honest and telling it like it is and having a great eye;

... Veronique, for your constructive criticism; I deleted three whole pages because of you!

... Kristin, for having such a good eye and asking me what a Love Jones is, and what Cisco was; I'm still laughing about that.

... Faizah, for your quick-witted humor and allowing me to use some of it in the book;

... LaShanta, for being so passionate about "my" voice;

... Jones family, in advance, for your support and understanding during my journey.

... Ramya, I have page numbers!

I could not have done this without you.

To

Aisha, Amari, and Malik

I love you.

When Life Becomes

A Love Story

EBAN
"fence"

Symbol of love, safety, and security

The home to the Akan is a special place. A home that has a fence around it is considered to be an ideal residence.

The fence symbolically separates and secures the family from the outside. Because of the security and the protection that a fence affords, **_the symbol is also associated with the security and safety one finds in love._**

-- from *The Adinkra Dictionary*

Track 1

Storm Gon' Come

I've been through the storm.
I'm a bit more tattered and a whole lot worn.
I haven't had the easiest way.
Just tried to make it another day.
I was beaten and kicked and tossed about.
Didn't know if I had the strength to make it out.
Wasn't prepared for such a long fight
While searching for the answers to the questions of
life.
Made some mistakes, I took a detour or two.
Try not to judge me till you've walked in my shoes.
The rain has passed and now it's calm.
I still have bad days. Don't get me wrong.
So when dark clouds come rolling in,
And I smell the scent of rain again,

I ball my fists ready to fight,
Clinch my teeth with all my might.
But my *eban* is built and it shields me
From the pain and shame that haunts me
I'm stronger now; it's not the same.
I open my arms and welcome the rain.
Because the rain has come to wash away
All the heartache the fear and the pain.

"Ayo, are you sure you can handle this responsibility?" Mom asked.

"Yes," I said. "Have faith in me."

In fact, I was scared. I'd just moved back to my mother's home in Alexandria from Virginia Beach and I'd only been gone for a year this time. I'd left to manage a startup youth program. I'd been doing well until the contract ended. It wasn't the first time I'd lost a job due to a program losing its funding, but I was determined it would be the last. I hadn't wanted to move back, but I had no savings. This was the third time I'd had to return home since leaving my now ex-husband thirteen years earlier, and Mom had made it very clear that she wouldn't stand for my moving back anymore. The last time I'd moved home, I stayed a wee bit longer than either of us had anticipated and it put a lot of stress on our relationship. I swore then I'd never move back again. Did I say never?

My daughter was almost sixteen years old then and I was still struggling with self-sufficiency. Mom was retiring the following year, in June 2007, and moving to Tennessee. She was allowing me to take over her mortgage. I had three years to get my finances together to buy her house or start looking for another place to live. In the meantime, I also had to take care of the utilities, trash collection, and yard maintenance. It was a bit overwhelming. The yard was

❖

huge and I'd already done a lot of landscaping. I'd laid terracotta tiles in the living room, installed a sink and toilet in the upstairs bathroom, stripped and re-stained floors, and there was still much to do.

Don't get me wrong. I made a good living as a corporate trainer, but northern Virginia is expensive. I'm a single mother of two. I take care of my 15-year-old daughter Kaiya and my 11-year-old nephew Tariq. I lived about fifteen minutes from Washington, DC and Maryland, in a beautiful, tree-lined, working class neighborhood, where all the split-level houses look the same, and I couldn't ask for a better school district. But they sure make you pay for all this beauty.

I had to pay property taxes on a car that I could barely afford to maintain and, even though gas prices were at an all-time high, it cost me more to take public transportation to work than it did to drive and pay one hundred dollars a month for parking. I'd been considering riding my bike to work, but really didn't have much of a choice.

I lived like most working poor. If one thing happened that wasn't part of my budget at the beginning of the month, I'd be looking for a place to live by the end of the month. I earned enough to cover the mortgage on one check and most of the living expenses on the other. Life got in the way sometimes. My daughter had dental braces to correct her crooked teeth and a back brace to correct her curved spine, and I was behind on payments for both. The creditors kept threatening to report me to the credit bureaus, but I was past caring. As far as I was concerned, they could've taken a pair of pliers to her teeth and repossessed her back brace. Meanwhile, she'd just lost her Baby Phat transitional lenses.

Kaiya's father hasn't paid any support since she was five years old. For the longest time, I wanted to believe that he would send support when and if he could. But, finally, I had to go to court.

I've had my youngest sister, Shani's, son Tariq, since he was two. Now, he's eleven and needs new everything. He's ripped every pair of his pants at the knees and his shoes smell so bad that he has to keep them outside. My sister helps when she's able. But right now she ain't able.

Tariq doesn't ask for much. That's the beauty of raising a tween boy. His needs are simple. He's as happy and clueless as a pig in a poke, but I hate that he looks forgotten sometimes. His mom tries but misses the mark quite often. She'll buy clothes for him, but by the time she gets around to sending them – sometimes as much as three years later – he's outgrown them. And at this very moment I'm watching him eat me out of house and home.

I was tired of struggling and so, with Mom leaving, I decided that there was only one thing to do: get a boarder to help with the bills, like my best friend Regina in Orlando did. She could hustle her way out of any financial bind. I didn't want to put an ad in the paper because I was afraid of what I'd get. The boarder would have to be family or someone who was close enough to be family.

I ran down the list of everyone I knew. There was so much to think about, like my daughter being fifteen and extremely moody, and my nephew's inability to pick up after himself without constant reminding. I wanted someone who could do minor repairs around the house. After all, the windows required weather proofing and the drywall on the ceiling in my nephew's room cried out for

❖

replacement because of considerable water damage. So there was a lot I needed in a boarder.

Most of all I needed someone I could trust.

The only person I could think of was Brandon. He'd been a family friend for more than ten years. I met him while living in Orlando. He was the maintenance guy at my apartment. He was involved in a couple of car accidents a few years ago and was forced to move back in with his parents. He lived in a home office off the side of their house that wasn't much larger than the twin-sized blow up mattress he slept on. He was applying for disability and awaiting a settlement from his second accident. Perfect. I expected him to come up after Mom relocated but his story was so sad Mom suggested he come immediately.

It took about four months of constant emailing and phone calls to convince him to relocate up North from Orlando. I didn't blame his hesitation. I wouldn't have made the move if I'd known I was going to struggle the same way I did down there, despite making more than an additional twenty-five thousand dollars a year.

Brandon warned me that he looked different. I knew he walked with a cane and had let his hair grow past his shoulders, but other than that, I had no idea how he looked and frankly didn't care. I needed help with some of these bills. He was a bit of a neat freak, which worried me, but he would have his own room to escape to.

He took a 24-hour train ride up because he was too paranoid about a terrorist attack to take a plane, even though it had been more than five years since 9/11. He arrived on Christmas Day, 2006. When I saw him get off that train, I almost got back into my car

❖

and left him at the station. He looked like a vagabond and smelled worse. He wore mirrored sunglasses, a full beard and about two feet of frizzy hair sticking up all over his head.

He'd traveled from Florida, so I could understand why he only wore a white T-shirt, but it was about forty-five degrees that day. He was lucky that global warming had delayed the snow. His jeans hung halfway down the crack of his ass, but it was his limbs that scared me. His right leg flew out to the side as he walked and his left hand was twisted as if he'd had a mild stroke. I thought about that episode of "Good Times" when Michael brought home Ned the wino. After they scrubbed Ned down, he looked decent enough for his wife to want to take him home. So I told myself that Brandon just needed a good scrubbing. I just hoped I had soap strong enough.

I know I told him I needed help with the house. How was he going to help me if his arms and legs didn't work? I began to worry that instead of a boarder, I'd simply gotten another mouth to feed.

The first couple of months were okay. We caught up on old times. He made breakfast and dinner for everyone every day. Our arrangement worked well: he was picking up my slack. Because of his disability, it took him three weeks to complete the drywall in Tariq's room, but I didn't mind because the room had been in that state for ten years. Brandon made other home repairs that had been neglected as well.

At night, he cried about being unable to work and in constant pain. I suggested that he see a counselor, which he did. The psychiatrist prescribed medication for Brandon's depression and pain and he seemed to get better. He enjoyed the change. He wasn't hustling a stranger in front of the gas station or

❖

his mother for that matter for beer or cigarette money. Moreover, he was sleeping in his own comfortable bed in his own room.

He connected with some estranged aunts and uncles that lived in Maryland. That was big for him because he'd held a grudge against them ever since he was fourteen. He blamed them for causing his family to have such a hard time when they moved to this country from Trinidad. He used to tell me about them when we met and swore he'd never talk to them again. I guess his heart was healed because he happily reacquainted himself with aunts and uncles, cousins and a visiting grandmother he hadn't seen in more than twenty years. He was happy and I was happy to have someone to help me.

After about seven months, he suggested that we try to make it as a couple and not just be roommates. I thought about it. We did have a history and I felt like I could grow to love him. It had been about two years since I'd last tried dating and had decided to give up on the idea. Neither of us thought we'd ever find our true loves, so we decided to settle for each other.

He was my second attempt at dating a disabled man. Since the accident Brandon was numb on one side of his body and suffered from erectile dysfunction. It took way too much effort on my part to make anything happen. I wasn't willing to work that hard anymore, so I only tried three more times to be intimate with him and was done. I wasn't in shape like I used to be and it wasn't fun. But it really didn't matter because as soon as I agreed to his proposal, he unzipped his mask to reveal a paranoid schizophrenic drug addict.

Brandon had decided that marijuana made him feel better than his medication did, especially since he

❖

could get it whenever he wanted to from his new favorite uncles. One uncle sold him three hundred dollars worth of New York Skank on a take home/pay later agreement. I've never heard of anyone being able to buy weed with no money down, like he was buying furniture or something. When I asked Brandon where he was going to get the money to pay his uncle he looked at me as if I was the dummy.

The night before his grandmother flew back to Trinidad, we went to visit her. She suffered from Alzheimer's and the relatives were talking as if this might be the last time they'd see her. We fought about his smoking on the way up, but he brought more weed home, anyway. I told him he couldn't handle the herb and fulfill his responsibilities around the house because it made him sleep all day. He tried to tell me his stress level was up because he might not see his grandmother again after having her back in his life again. I reminded him that I was the one who sat on the couch all night with his grandmother's head in my lap while he and his uncle smoked out back. I couldn't believe that after ten years of friendship he tried to play me like that.

Even with Mom in the house, Brandon made no effort to hide his irrational behavior. Mom overheard our arguments and noticed that I was making dinner again, but she didn't say anything. In fact, she rarely spoke to me about anything anymore, unless, of course, something bothered her so much that she couldn't stand it anymore. Then, she would go off. Three years ago, I knew I'd overstayed my welcome when, on the day before my 34th birthday, she exploded, telling me how much she disapproved of the way I disciplined my kids and mismanaged my money, and that I hadn't changed since I was a kid. I

❖

suppose she expected me to filter the advice from the insults, but I was too wounded to do so. I tucked those words away and tried to forget about them just like I'd always done. I knew she didn't like talking to me that way, but she didn't know any other.

Brandon began having paranoid episodes. He would conceal himself behind the bushes in the front yard and watch our neighbors' comings and goings. He'd jerk awake out of a sound sleep with night terrors, ranting and raving about who knows what. Once, he punched me in my head. I'm really not sure if that was a night terror or an excuse to hit me. When he got upset, he'd slam his head against walls and he never remembered what happened the next day. One time, the kids left the front door ajar before going to bed and he went off so bad, I thought I was going to have to call 911. Then I found out he was a Wiccan. I was finding crystals, candles, small bundled fibers and other paraphernalia used in modern day witchcraft hidden all over my house.

He started looking like a vagabond and not taking showers again. I decided to look up the medication he'd been prescribed by his psychiatrist because his behavior scared me to death. The label on the medication said it was used "to reduce psychotic episodes."

I gave him an ultimatum: take the medication or get out. He took the medication for a few days but complained it made him sick. It only made him sick because he mixed vodka and weed with it.

I refused to support his drug habit and wasn't going to allow him to stay around my kids with his volatile personality. And he certainly wasn't going to sit around playing video games all day, especially since I couldn't. I told him to make a choice. He didn't

❖

say a word. He developed a stare that he wouldn't break for hours.

Fed up, I finally asked him why he hadn't warned me about his illness. He tried to sound pitiful and reminded me that he'd said he had problems. Problems? No, I have problems. He, on the other hand, had serious life threatening issues!

Even though he couldn't stand talking to his mom, he got her to feel sorry for him. She pleaded with me, telling me that if his medication made him sick he shouldn't take it. I knew she didn't have all the details, so I let her state her case for him and left it alone. I wanted to tell her to come get him, but I knew that wasn't going to happen. She was happy to see him gone and he swore he'd rather go to a shelter than back to her house.

Shortly after, I started getting threatening phone calls from a girl in Orlando. She told me she'd met Brandon in a psych ward. They were supposed to be getting married and he used to smoke crack with her.

Psych ward? Crack? How had she gotten my number? He actually fixed his lips to tell me that his mom must have given it to her. I asked him to call his mother and tell her not to give out my number anymore. He called and pretended to do what I asked, but I knew he was full of it. Later that evening, he started crying again and admitted that he'd called this girl himself. He said he was sorry and that it wouldn't happen again.

It didn't take long for me to realize that crying was his way of trying to manipulate me. I also realized that he'd been having more than friendly communication with an old high school girlfriend on the Internet. He couldn't explain the half-naked

❖

pictures he'd downloaded on my computer. The only good thing about his drug use was that it made him careless and he couldn't get away with anything. After a couple of weeks of non-stop crazy, our short, not-quite-a-love affair was over.

A few weeks later, Mom moved to her new home to start the new phase of her life and Brandon really cut up. He moped around the house and refused to speak to anybody for days at a time. Everyone was uncomfortable. He stopped cooking and cleaning.

On Fridays, I would buy pizza for the house and he would eat more than half of it, suffering from the munchies. Sometimes I wouldn't eat so my kids could get full. When I confronted him about his behavior, he'd turn belligerent and try to intimidate me.

Once, he knocked the thermostat off the wall and threw my belongings around. Another time, he knocked a box of cereal off the counter and kept walking. I was so angry I picked up that box and hit him upside the back of his head with it. I'd seen Brandon angry, but not like that time. He turned on me like he was going to hurt me.

"Hit me and you're going to jail," I shouted.

He thought twice about it and, instead of stomping me, stomped the hell out of a brand new family-sized box of Cheerios.

He was absolutely certifiable. It didn't take him long to smoke three hundred dollars worth of herb and threw more fits because I wouldn't buy him more. Twice he left the house half-packed after I insisted that he either participate in the family life or get out. He made it a block up the street and then, after he saw that I wasn't going to chase him down, he called me in tears and asked me to pick him up. I found him sitting

❖

on the curb with crocodile tears running down his face, like he'd just lost his best friend. If it weren't for his mom calling me every week to check up on him he'd been gone.

I never knew what was real. He tried everything to get me to feel sorry for him. He even told me that he was fine until his mom took him to see a voodoo priestess back in Trinidad when he was five years old. She tried to shake the demons out of him, he said. A psychic had told her that her son would cause her pain. Well, the psychic was right, but the voodoo priestess must've been a quack because he's still full of demons.

He finally got the settlement check I was waiting for. It was only three thousand dollars but we needed it badly. After nine months of living with us and paying no bills, he had the audacity to spend $1,000 plus the $300 dollars he smoked previously on more weed. It took everything I had not to dropkick him in his bad hip.

He pretended to ignore me after I told him to get a job by that next Friday or he would be out. The next day he came to me excited about a newspaper sales position he'd found online. I was so relieved. Finally, he would start contributing to the house and things would be normal.

The nice part about his job was that he had cash in his pocket every day. He traveled though, which meant he dropped me off at work and I had to take the bus home. I didn't care about the inconvenience until I tried asking him for money for groceries or bus fare. He would pinch off his wad and give me five or ten dollars after boasting about making $200 that day. I didn't fight about it but I knew he had to go.

❖

The next day, my daughter told me she was unhappy and that Brandon was stressing her out. That was the last straw. I was trying to wait until he had saved enough money to get his own place, but I wasn't going to sacrifice my kids' happiness waiting. That evening, when he came home, I told him he had to leave by the end of the week. He got smart with me. I don't even remember what he said. I just told him to get out that night and to make sure that he left my cell phone on the table. As soon as I said that, I knew I wasn't going to see my phone again. Looking me directly in the eye, he took my cell phone out of his pocket and then, in a slow exaggerated motion, raised his hand high and slammed the phone to the floor.

While I picked up a million tiny little pieces, he called his brother, using the house phone. Brandon was crying as usual, but I wasn't having it. I sent the kids to the neighbors and went to the police station to file a report. I was scared that the situation might even get worse, especially if he found out that I'd thrown away the marijuana plant he'd been growing on the windowsill.

When I got back, he was on the patio laughing on the phone with his brother. He was startled to see me.

"Are you ready to go?" I asked.

His smile vanished. He stayed out a couple of more hours, making frantic phone calls and crying some more. When he finally came back inside, he was a bit more humble.

He asked if he could leave in the morning. I was hesitant. I was scared of what he might do in the middle of the night, but felt I had no choice. The police had said I could do nothing about my cell phone or kicking him out. They'd said that if Brandon

❖

didn't leave on his own, I'd have to have him evicted, which could take three months. I needed him to believe that I had the upper hand.

He took every available blanket and sheet in that house and made a pallet on the living room floor. He was so dramatic. When the kids came home, they asked me why Brandon was crying and sleeping on the floor. I told them that he was sad because he couldn't live with us anymore.

I slept with one eye open that night.

The next day, Brandon packed his belongings. I followed him around the house. I didn't want him to break something else or take something that didn't belong to him. I didn't have much but he managed to break a microwave, a vacuum, and a few other things I still can't afford to replace.

"Where is it?" he asked.

I knew he wanted his plant but I played dumb. He was pissed. He walked around the house, gathering his belongings, and I followed, begging him not to break anything else. He rambled on about how I would regret everything. I already regretted everything.

"I've been expecting this to happen," he said. "So, you know what? I've been setting you up for months. You can expect social services. You're going to loose those kids. I made sure of that."

His uncle pulled into the driveway and Brandon left. He couldn't pack the car quickly enough. As soon as he left I locked the door behind him and screamed a sigh of relief loud enough for him to hear. Brandon and his uncle sat in the driveway for a while and I got nervous. I found a pencil and paper, and wrote down the license plate number. After what seemed like an eternity, they drove off.

❖

I knew he was crazy and that business about setting me up was just crazy talk, but there was no telling what he was capable of. I've been nervous ever since. My house sits on about a fourth of an acre, with a lot of bushes and trees. He could have planted seeds all over my yard and I wouldn't know it. Months later, I would realize that he had planted at least one seed and it was fertilized. Damn!

I felt better after he left but I still needed more income. Another roommate was out of the question. My student loan company was threatening to garnish my wages at the end of the month. My dentist was suing me; Kaiya's back brace was in collections; I owed money to Tariq's ear doctor and I couldn't take the boy back until I paid.

The only thing saving me was a refund from my income tax return, but soon that would be gone. I wasn't about to call Mom for help; Antonio still refused to pay child support; and my sister was unemployed. That roommate situation with Brandon didn't start or end quite the way I wanted it to. I've never been a good hustler.

After Brandon left, I had flashbacks of when he flirted with the ladies at my company's holiday party, or threw up and passed out at his uncle's bar-b-que and I laughed hysterically.

Once I composed myself, I sat down to take a good look at the choices I'd made. Why had I always allowed friends and family to do and say whatever hurtful things they wanted to, while I absorbed all of their toxins? I thought about why I continued to make the same mistakes, felt worthless and alone. Not only did I need to understand, but I also needed to cleanse myself so I could finally be free.

❖

I wrote to express myself. I cried when the hurt became overwhelming, I screamed when I wanted to fight and I fought when the screaming wasn't enough. I disassociated for my sanity. I drank when I didn't want to feel and I suppressed when my mind couldn't take anymore.

I used to think my hell started when I met my ex-husband. Upon reflection, I realized that my issues stemmed from experiences that occurred long before that. He was a symptom of my pain.

Through self-reflection, I confronted years of pain and reviewed personal choices. I forced myself to relive painful memories, memories I'd tried to forget. I'd been miserable for most of my life because I was too ashamed to tell anyone, even those closest to me, that I needed help or that I was hurting. During my journey, I learned to let go of my shame and I realized that there were people who wanted to help me. Finally, I was able to release the pain that had been locked away like a caged beast.

I used to think that being alone was the best place for me to be because that was where I was most comfortable. It was where the only disappointing eyes I saw were my own.

I understand now that my issues are my own and that my troubles are not the result of what others had done to me. I saw how I allowed other people to dictate my happiness. I realized that I suffered from emotional bondage and that it was up to me to break the chains. I knew that I needed to find a way to believe in myself, despite feeling like I'd always be a failure. I knew that I allowed my fear of disappointing others to dictate my actions; that my desire to feel love blinded my reality; and that I couldn't see when I was being taken advantage of. I understood that I'd

❖

often looked for quick fixes for my issues without believing that with time I could fix them; that I jumped from job to job and state to state, thinking that life would be better somewhere else. I needed an eban, a word for fence, used by the Akan people of Ghana. They believe a home with a fence is a special place. It's associated with the protection, support and security one finds in love.

Once I was done writing, I realized that I was in control of my happiness and of whom I allowed into my life. I had to realize that I chose to let in certain people, people who weren't capable of giving love to begin with – and that if I made a mistake in trusting the wrong person and they hurt me, then I still had a say as to how I handled the pain.

Afterward, I felt better. My fear had turned to joy. I looked down at my belly and smiled. I now knew that I would be just fine.

So what did it take for me to change the way I handled people when they tried to wreak havoc in my life?

Only losing the love I thought would complete me, emotionally separating myself from some relatives and allowing lifelong friends to be there for me.

❖

Track 2

My First

I was just glad to know you,
To call you my very own.
For so many years,
I thought I'd walk this path alone.
You were my first,
My everything.
You showed me love and affection,
And in return,
I gave you my most precious gift.
But as time went on,
I don't think it was really love
But more infatuation
Because when I looked into those your eyes of yours
All I saw was my imagination.
I'm not sure what I ever saw in you

Or what we had in common.
We didn't share the same hopes or dreams.
I was so in love with the idea of love
And wasn't strong enough to let you go
Because you were my first,
My everything.

I grew up in a single-parent household with Mom, whose name is Fannie, Grandma Esther and two sisters. My sisters and I were each three years apart. Naja was the oldest. She was tall and athletic, like a model, with perfect hair. Shani was the baby; she had flawless skin, beautiful thick, black hair and was a little on the chubby side. She was adopted from my cousin when she was three days old. I was the middle child; I was short and skinny and suffered from the typical middle child syndrome. I had no sense of belonging, was riddled with insecurities and was very opinionated.

My father lived only six blocks from our home in St. Louis, but he didn't play an active role in raising me. He taught art at Central Visual and Performing Arts High School, and was a gun-toting member of the National Rifle Association and an ex-Marine who loved discussing politics.

Mom was quiet, calm, and strong. She was a proud intellectual and well spoken. She didn't allow anyone in her business or involve herself in theirs. She didn't allow us to speak slang at home. She got a scholarship to Harvard, but couldn't go because she had to provide for her family. Active in grass roots politics: participating in freedom rides, organizing voter registration drives and was an original member of the Oakland-based Black Panther Party.

❖

She set high standards for us and encouraged us to make our own decisions. Once, when I was about seven years old, I asked her if she thought I should throw away the peanut butter jar. She simply asked, "Do you think it should be thrown away? Can you get any more peanut butter out of the jar?" I remember standing there, wishing she'd confirm whether I'd made the right decision, but she wouldn't. Mom taught us to have our own opinions and to question everything.

Also, she never spanked us. Aunt Sealy, on the other hand, never spared the rod. She couldn't stand me. "Stay in a child's place and out of grown folks face," she'd say. She was old school and preferred kids to be seen, not heard.

Mom worked two jobs to keep us fed and clothed, and to pay for a live-in nanny and private schools. She involved us in sports and cultural events. Every year, she invited international students to stay with us. I got my work ethic, generosity, bull-headed pride, and need for privacy from her. In short, she imparted a great deal to me, but as with many homes where one parent does the job of two, some things were missing. We didn't enjoy special mother-daughter talks. There weren't talks about boys or sex. We didn't begin our days with "Good morning" or end them with "I love you." I don't remember hugs or tender moments. I felt physically safe but my emotional needs weren't met.

I had a great experience growing up in St. Louis. I grew up in a historic district in a three-story brick house with a full basement that Mom bought for $20,000. Stained glass windows decorated the second-floor landing. A butler's pantry separated the dining room and kitchen. Three fireplaces heated the

❖

house and the garage had room for three cars. My sisters and I enjoyed our own rooms and bountiful Christmases. We used to live in a smaller house in University City, a suburb of St. Louis until the white flight of the 1970s.

I remember penny candy from the corner store and jumping Double Dutch with the neighbors. When it rained, my sisters and I would put on our bathing suits and stand under the gutters. I remember Grandma's homemade biscuits, made with oleo and potlikker. We'd put cornbread in a cup and pour collard greens juice over it, and then eat it with a spoon. In winter, she would put vanilla extract in our bowls of freshly fallen snow.

Before attending church, my sisters and I would sit on the edge of the bed and Grandma would grease us down with Vaseline before we put on our Sunday best. Once, while we waited for the church bus to pick us up, Naja put on her Michael Jackson LP and Grandma threw a fit. "You don't listen to that devil music on the Lord's day!" I remember Grandma's expressions of speech like, "Turn yo' shirt hind proppa foe", which meant that we had our shirts on backwards.

The first and last time my father was invited to Thanksgiving dinner I was eight. Grandma knew he was an atheist but insisted he say grace anyway.

"Thank-you for the invitation; lets eat!"

Then he broke the circle of hands and headed to the buffet to fix his plate. Grandma and Great Aunt Jessie Mae stood mortified. The rest of us bowed our heads, took the hand of the person on either side of us and tried not to laugh for the next twenty-five minutes while they sang and hummed hymns, to rebuke my dad's blasphemy.

I also remember the not-so-great stuff like when Grandma found a rifle and drug paraphernalia on her paper route, or when the candy lady was kidnapped and held at gunpoint in her home. I remember having to walk past Cabanne Courts, the fifth most dangerous housing projects in the country at that time, to go to church, and hearing that there had been multiple shootings at a house down the street. I remember the time a strange man followed my friends and me around in his car while he fondled himself, and how a neighbor chased us with a BB gun after we'd teased him too much.

A few things worked against me growing up. In the '70s, I wore a short, nappy fro, while other girls my age were wearing press and curls. In the early '80s, I kept my cornrows in way too long, so there was always a halo of thick, fresh growth about a half-inch high all over my head. In 1984, when I was thirteen, Mom finally took me to get a relaxer. My hair was nice for about five weeks. She didn't realize that once you got a relaxer, you had to get your roots touched up every six to eight weeks. By the eighth week, I had a short nappy fro again, but this time only in the back where the straightened hair had broken off. I was so happy the Jheri Curl had been invented.

My waistline was larger than my breast size, which never grew past an "A" cup. I had a bad case of acne, a sway back, and narrow hips. I was an ugly little girl. I knew it and I knew everyone else knew it. So when a cute guy finally took interest in me, it went to my head. That was all it took to turn every last one of my future career goals into a distant memory.

But I'm getting ahead of myself.

Mom had every career in the book. She was a medical technologist in the Air Force for six years, ten

❖

months and twenty-one days. After she left the military she was a medical technologist at several civilian hospitals and the St. Louis Zoo Hospital. After she received her Masters Degree in Education she became an Assistant Professor of Education at Harris Stowe State College.

In 1985, Mom left her "good government job at the VA," as her friends used to say, and her second job selling insurance, to open an ice cream parlor. She worked from dawn to dusk to salvage the business. But a year later she had to close it down because the employees had constantly stolen her profits and the cops put the shakedown on her. At first, she told the cops that she didn't need "protection." Right after that, a man wearing a stocking cap walked up to the drive-through window and brandished a 22-gauge shotgun. However, he didn't take any money and we realized that his visit was meant to scare us. So Mom hired the off-duty cops again, and we had no more problems of that ilk.

Mom took a job at Ft. Leonard Wood Army Post as an Education Specialist. She taught leadership and management courses and the International Student Orientation Course. We moved to Waynesville, a small town two and a half hours west of St. Louis. I was a sophomore in high school by then. Waynesville had one main road, Historic Rt. 44. It couldn't have been more rural and different from St. Louis. No more Double Dutch and no more hanging out on the front steps talking about a whole lot of nothing with my friends. Instead, I got Ku Klux Klan rallies and Piggly Wiggly, a popular grocery store in rural areas.

My walk to school took me past a little rickety house that belonged to the Wickles family. Thirteen

❖

kids lived in that tiny two-room house. All were mentally delayed except for one. Rumor had it that the parents were sister and brother. The mom and kids were extremely thin, but the father weighed more than three hundred and fifty pounds. I walked as quietly as I could past that house because, if they spotted me, they would lean out of their window and yell, "Hey nigger, nigger, nigger." It scared me to death. At school later that day, those same kids would pass me in the hall and act like nothing had ever happened.

My school serviced mostly military kids. I was used to going to school where I was only one of two black kids because I was a victim of the court-sanctioned desegregation program that St. Louis implemented back in the mid '80s. I had to take a test to prove that I was smart enough to handle their curriculum. Mom had told me stories and I'd watched programs on PBS during Black History Month, so I knew the world thought blacks were different, but knowing and experiencing are two different things.

When I was bused to the county to get a "better education," I met with Mr. Jim Crow himself. I was smart enough for the new school's curriculum but I wasn't mature enough to handle the attention. The white kids would ask me if I washed my hair or say that I didn't talk or act like black people. They would ask why black parents spanked their kids. They would tell me that black people were good at being funny and order me to make them laugh. Intimidated, I answered their questions and told racial jokes that confirmed their stereotypes. I felt like Little Black Sambo and I resented being their sideshow.

The one nice thing about my new school was that I wasn't the only minority in my class anymore. It

❖

included Asians, Native Americans and Polynesians, as well as white and black American kids. I still stood out, though: I didn't have the best clothes, still had "bad" hair and was battling a face full of acne.

I met Antonio, the cute guy I mentioned, in the summer of '89, the year I graduated from high school. He was a tall, lanky private in the military. His hair was cut in a high top fade. Standing 5'9" and weighing 129 lbs, he had caramel-colored skin and light brown eyes. He was from Morganton, North Carolina and had never been outside of Morganton before. He had an obvious naïve and simple way about him, even more than I did, which was how we ended up together.

Antonio was supposed to have been set up with my best friend, Tettie, a quick-witted, abrasive Texan. She would make fun of you and laugh right in your face. Anything could set her off: your shoes, your having tripped over a rock, or the car your mother drove. No one could stand her, except her sister and me, and half the time I couldn't stand her either. She'd publicly humiliated me many times. I only dealt with her because, if I hadn't, I wouldn't have had a social life. Well, she said something to Antonio that turned him off. That left him free to go out with me.

Antonio and I couldn't get enough of each other. Mom noticed that I was spending a lot of time with him, but when I didn't come home at night, the only thing she said was, "I don't think what you're doing is a good idea." That was like telling a crack addict to stop hitting the pipe because it might be harmful to his health. She was afraid to say anything, fearful that I would react negatively and become even more involved with Antonio. As a parent, I know how

❖

hard it is to tell your kids something they don't want to hear. But I sure wish she had.

That was the best summer of my life. By the time I graduated, I had my acne under control. I was working at McDonalds and could buy myself better clothes. I went from watching TV on Saturday nights to clubbing, hanging out at the park and drinking malt liquor with the cool crowd, to finally having a boyfriend. We had the same routine every weekend. I'd pick up my girls from post, drive off post to the car wash where we flirted with all the guys and then go back on post to hang out at the park. Antonio had the loudest system in his car. I loved being the girl sitting on the hood of the car, playing the loudest music and watching all the haters go by.

The summer ended way too soon and I had to go off to college. It was difficult to leave Antonio and all of my friends. I'd been the only one in our circle with career goals, and by then I wanted to stay and party with them. I remember sitting in the parking lot by the barracks, crying for about twenty minutes, wishing I didn't have to go.

The next morning, I drove the nine hours to Holly Springs, Mississippi. Things were great in college. I was on the Dean's List, and made some really good friends. I aced all of my classes, gained academic recognition, and felt good about myself. I wanted to become a psychiatrist, fill stadiums with lost souls, and lead them to a new life. I wanted to save the world.

Like-minded people surrounded me. You would think that would've been enough, but something was missing. I couldn't stop thinking about my boyfriend. He'd needed five years to make it out of

❖

high school, instead of the traditional four, and had atrocious grammar.

Antonio drove all the way to Mississippi to visit me before he was deployed to fight in Desert Storm. I paraded him around campus, making sure all of my friends saw him. We rented a room from the local roach motel and had the kind of sex that 19-year-olds are especially good at: hot, long, and raw. You know the kind, where you go at it for hours and the longer you do it, the better it gets. I believe our longest was seven hours. We tried every night to set new personal records. Nothing was more important to me than being with him.

After Antonio left, I got the same kinds of comments I did growing up in St. Louis. Back then, my friends would say, "Your sister's so pretty. What happened to you?" I remember a conversation I had with my sister Naja after she'd graduated from college. She worked in the entertainment industry and I shared with her that I wanted to be an actress. She told me that they wanted a different kind of look. She hesitated and tried not to sound like she was calling me ugly. In a conversation with Mom, I expressed my desire to go to a performing arts college; she suggested that I get a 'practical degree' instead. Those comments, along with other life-altering childhood experiences, were the reasons why I was in Mississippi studying psychology and not in New York or California studying theater arts.

In college, I would get more comments like, "He's so cute," along with a puzzled-looked that clearly said they didn't understand why a cute man like him would be out with a girl like me. They didn't realize their words worked to crush my spirit. Actually, I didn't realize it either, not until years later.

❖

I met Lei during that first year in college. We became best friends the day we met. We had both just experienced our first boyfriends, so we had much to talk about. Whenever we had money, we'd walk up to the local liquor store and buy cheap wine. We'd get drunk and end up laughing hysterically on the campus lawn in front of the boys' dorm. She invited me home to spend the Christmas holidays with her family. Her parents, Alfonza and Savannah were very demonstrative. They showered me with hugs, kisses and I love you's. I envied their relationship. They held hands at the dinner table and everyone had to say a prayer. I yearned for this kind of family relationship. At the same time, it made me uncomfortable because I wasn't used to it.

I created reasons to be miserable. The dorms were too small and the bathrooms were nasty. The food was even worse, but I still managed to gain fifteen pounds during my freshman year. Right before Christmas of my sophomore year, I got into an argument with my roommates about our messy dorm room and lack of space. It was the last straw. I transferred to a state college an hour away from home. One of the real reasons for the move was to get back to Antonio, but he'd been deployed by the time I made it.

My grades plunged. I went from a small college with small classrooms to a large university with auditorium-style lectures given over a public announcement system. I was lost in a sea of kids who had already bonded and created cliques. I tried walking around campus to see what the happenings were. I visited the student union and other social areas, only to be ignored despite attempting to make eye contact and smiling at anyone who looked

❖

approachable. I soon withdrew to the safety of my room and spent the rest of the semester there. I was there so much that my roommate asked me to leave sometimes so she and her boyfriend could have time alone. I wished I were back in Holly Springs with my friends, but it was too late.

Instead, I ended up back at home with Mom. The transfer had screwed up my student loan and I had flunked all of my classes. Mom thought I'd messed up on purpose. I could see the disgust on her face. She never said much to me but she didn't have to. Her facial expressions spoke volumes. I've always felt like a disappointment and to this day I avoid eye contact with her as much as possible. I passed my time by taking classes on the post, working at Dairy Queen, and writing Antonio every day.

Since most of our boyfriends were away fighting, my girlfriends and I occupied our time by hanging out at the gym and the bowling alley. We'd also sneak into the NCO Club. That was the most fun. Some drunken guy would open a locked door in the back of the club and we'd sneak into the bathroom and ask some drunken woman to rub the back of her hand against ours to transfer the neon stamp. When I wasn't getting kicked out of the club, I was glued to the television, watching CNN's non-stop coverage of the war. I'd study images of the troops, hoping to get a glimpse of Antonio.

Six months later, he and I were reunited. The soldiers arrived home in the spring of 1991 to a heroes welcome. Mist dampened the air and the hairstyle that I'd worked on for two hours was ruined by humidity in five minutes. It was a dramatic scene as twenty black and tan luxury buses paraded down the main road, their hoods glistening under the

❖

streetlights. One by one, the soldiers made a grand entrance through the gymnasium doors to the joyful cries of family members from all over the country. When I saw Antonio, I burst into tears. I never wanted to spend another day without him again. As soon as formation broke, I ran into his arms and we picked up right where we'd left off.

At least, I thought we had.

Antonio came back a different person. He wanted to do things without me. He'd never been that way before. Now, he was more independent. He needed to explore life, as any young man would, without his girl in tow. I, on the other hand, had become much, much clingier.

Our relationship was about two-and-a-half years old. I had staked everything on it, and when it began to fail, I couldn't handle it. For months, we argued about him not being where I could find him. The pivotal moment came when I threatened to break up with him if he went to North Carolina with one of his friends. I refused to let him go out of town to party without me after his disappearing acts. We fought for hours and after everything was said and done, we pretended to have "break up" sex.

We'd always taken precautions not to get pregnant until that night. Truth is I knew as much as he did that in that moment of desperation our lives would be connected forever.

❖

Track 3

Volatile Affair

There's a precious life in my belly
And it grows stronger every day.
So please don't hurt my baby,
I beg you and I pray.
You can do what you want to me,
But she's all I have,
So please don't take her from me.
I beg you and I pray.
I've dreamt of having this family,
A dad, a mom, and a baby girl running about.
But if you put her in harms way again,
The daddy part we'll live without.

We were twenty-one and twenty-two years young and
expecting our first child. We played house and

attempted to create a home that neither of us had ever experienced. We got married a few months after I got pregnant. The marriage took place on March 17, 1992, I think. After we got the license from the courthouse, Antonio gave it to a soldier who was supposed to be an ordained minister. We thought the soldier signed the license that Friday. Months later, I realized that he hadn't signed it until the following Sunday. I've been confused about my actual anniversary ever since.

It's no wonder that our union would be plagued with difficulties. We never stood before God, our families, friends or each other for that matter to exchange any vows that would bind us as a couple. I don't even know if that soldier was legally empowered to sign those papers. His wife signed the marriage certificate as the witness and I'd never met her.

But this is all in hindsight. At the time, I was so excited to be starting my family with the man I loved. We moved into military-based housing. Our new home was a nice-sized, two-story, two-bedroom yellow duplex. It was identical to every other house on the base except for the color. We had little furniture – just a couple of mismatched, borrowed pieces – but we were comfortable. We did buy a heated waterbed that came in handy during the cold Missouri winters.

I was used to Antonio drinking daily, but he was drinking even more than usual. Because I was pregnant, our social life dramatically ended and the change was getting to him. I, at least, had my growing belly to take my mind off how our lives had changed. I concentrated on taking my prenatal vitamins, exercising, and visiting my doctor. I got lost in dreaming of my baby's first word, first steps, first day of school, and everything else first-time mothers daydream about.

❖

Antonio, on the other hand, was dealing with pressure from his boys about being whipped and not being able to go out and play. That was a big deal for a young macho soldier who was being forced out of the social scene. He was able to get lost in his love of cars for a while. He loved everything about them: customizing the paint, tinting them, washing them, and shining them. He spent hours detailing his pride and joy. Her name was Peaches and she was a forest green, 1985, 325e, BMW. He would spend sunup to sundown with his Betsy, and when the sun went down, he drank. He handled the constant taunting for a while, but eventually it became too much for him.

Antonio was usually a mild-mannered, patient, southern gentleman with me. I was boisterous, with a strong personality. I fought for what I wanted and usually won. But a few drinks of liquid courage made him brave enough to stand up to me. It didn't faze me at first. When he got loud, I got louder. When he couldn't get his way by yelling, he graduated to just walking out. He'd rather deal with my wrath later than deprive himself of any pleasure he desired.

As the months went by, he became braver. He took advantage of the fact that I had become considerably less combative as my pregnancy progressed. I was protective of our child and, even though Antonio didn't want me to be, I was protective of him as well.

One Saturday, he started drinking around three in the afternoon. He was tipsy by five and pissy drunk by seven. By ten o'clock that evening, he had decided to go to the club. I begged him not to drive in his condition. Usually he went with a group of his boys, but none of them showed up that evening. (Maybe, they'd grown tired of the angry stare I'd give them

❖

every time they came to take my husband away.) So Antonio would've been driving drunk and going off alone. Determined to stop him, I grabbed him. He pushed me away and got into the car. I jumped on the hood, thinking he wouldn't dare drive off, not with me on it. After all, I was eight months pregnant. He wouldn't put his child and me in danger. He might get out and pull me off, but he certainly wouldn't drive off.

I was so wrong.

He threw the car in reverse and sped up our winding street. I held on for dear life. It was dark and I couldn't see anything except periodic glimpses of his silhouette through the front windshield when he would pass under a streetlight. He knew I was there. He must've seen the fear on my face, but it didn't snap him back to reality. He must've been driving at least fifty-five miles an hour on our 15-mile an hour residential street. I was sliding from side to side, terrified that I would slide right off the hood. I prayed hard, prayed that something would happen to make him stop the car without killing us, or that someone would intervene.

And someone did.

Headlights flashed behind us and Antonio pulled over. A guy drove up beside us and said that the cops had been called. I suspected that he was one of the neighbors who had been watching us act as damn fools in the front yard all night. Trembling from head to foot, I got down off the hood and into our car.

Once we got home both of us refused to get out of the car. I convinced Antonio to trade places with me. I reminded him that if the MPs saw him in the driver's seat, they would arrest him. Their sirens and

❖

lights warned us long before they reached us and I thought about the lie I was going to tell.

When the MPs arrived, they knocked on the door of our house with the backs of their flashlights and tried to look through our windows. We didn't answer. I hoped they'd go away if no one answered. After about five minutes, the officers turned and walked toward the car. Antonio had put limo tint on the car windows so you couldn't see inside just by looking. One officer put his hand on the hood to feel the heat of the engine. He flashed his lights inside the windshield and there we were, frozen and wide-eyed as two 16-year-olds who had been caught with their pants down, terrified that their parents would find out. The officer shook his head in disgust, rolled his eyes and shouted at us to roll our windows down.

We denied everything and no one went to jail because, even though the interior of the care was thick with the smell of cheap booze and Antonio was slurring his words, I was the one sitting in the driver's seat.

After the MPs left, Antonio called someone to come and get him and I didn't see him again until three o'clock the next afternoon. After all of that, that jackass still left and I spent the night alone, crying myself to sleep.

That incident should have been a major life lesson for both of us, but it wasn't. Instead it would be the first of many life-threatening events I would find myself in because of Antonio's new love, Ms. Malt Liquor.

Things did calm down for the next few weeks. He didn't go out as much but entertained at the house. I was bigger than ever. It was the middle of August; it was hot and humid and my due date was the first of

❖

September. I felt fat and ugly. I was in no mood to entertain, but I went along and didn't object because it kept my husband at home. Our single and not so single friends would bring their flavors of the week and on days I hid in our bedroom Antonio misbehaved. He had his hands on random girl's knees or engaged in quiet conversation. I never told him that I witnessed his behavior, even though it made me furious.

After Kaiya was born, matters seemed to get back to where they were at the beginning of our relationship. We were happy. Antonio stayed home and I had new hope for our family.

❖

Track 4

He Cheated

The evidence was clear.
You cheated on me with another woman
When I wasn't here.
I was devastated, and irritated,
And in absolute disbelief
That our young relationship
Was tainted with infidelity.
I was naïve and full of hope
To think that one day
You'd find a way
To commit to me and stay.
But as time went on,
Was forever gone
The friend that I once knew.
But you didn't just cheat on me,

You cheated our daughter, too.
I disguised my pain behind a smile
In order to hide my shame.
The bruises are gone,
The scars have healed,
But emotionally I'm falling apart
Because of the blatant disregard you had
For us that tore our family apart.

In 1992, Antonio got stationed in Berlin and left that December. Kaiya and I followed a month later. I had a long time to think about what I wanted to do and to reflect on the last few months. I knew that I wanted to be married and promised myself that I would be a good wife. I thought that if I were nicer to him, he'd be nicer to me.

I was thrilled to be in another country, to be leaving our old life behind and getting a chance at a new beginning. The Berlin Wall had fallen just four years earlier and I really wanted to see East Berlin. I'd heard so many things about it but wanted to see for myself. I remember watching the chaos unfold on TV and hearing how different the East was from the West.

Our apartment house looked just like some of the housing projects in the United States. It was a tall, brick building of bland, unimpressive architecture, with rows and rows of cookie-cutter apartments, and no elevator. Our apartment was on the fifth floor, so I'd have to climb ten flights of stairs with a four-month-old baby every day. The laundry room was in the basement. How was I going to manage a new baby, a basket full of laundry and all those stairs? The upside was that our apartment was fully furnished, which made life really easy for us. There were dishes, dining room furniture, a couch, chairs, a wall unit and every other household item we might need.

❖

I walked around the apartment with Kaiya in my arms, showing her all of our new stuff. After twenty minutes of exploration, I found some items that most definitely weren't government-issued household goods: light brown, curly hairs. They were embedded in the sheets and pillowcases of our bed.

Apparently, Papa Bear didn't mind sharing his bed after all. My silly ass husband wasn't even smart enough to get rid of the evidence of his infidelity. There was so much hair that she'd either emptied her brush in the bed or she had been spending a lot of time there.

Overwhelmed and sickened, I had to lean against the wall for support so I wouldn't drop Kaiya. My knees buckled and I sagged to the floor, with one arm wrapped around Kaiya and the other arm hanging limp. I landed on my right side. I had to lay Kaiya down, so I gently placed her next to me. For the next ten minutes, I fought to regain my composure and decide what to do. Should I yell at him, plunge a knife into his back, or get back on the plane and go home?

In the end, I confronted him. He made up a story about having a party and some people crashing there while they sobered up. I let it slide. I convinced myself that with me there we would start over and he wouldn't see her again.

My handling of that incident was an eye-opener. A few months earlier, I would've gone to battle. Instead, I merely accepted. I'd gone from being a bossy, loud-mouthed know-it-all who wouldn't back down from any fight to someone who was walked over and disrespected. I never thought my life would take such a turn. I couldn't believe I had altered so much.

❖

I needed to change the sheets but we didn't have an additional set. My welcome home gift consisted of me washing the bedding that another woman had been screwing my husband on, and then having to sleep on it myself.

Determined to make the most of our new posting, I signed up for a German language class. I only learned to say a few things with confidence, but I could count my money well. I also took a tour of the former East. As we approached the Brandenburg Gate, I remember part of President Reagan's speech, "Mr. Gorbachev, open this gate! Mr. Gorbachev, tear down this wall!"

The East was drastically different from the West. Some of the apartment buildings had twenty floors and no elevator, and the people living in them had to share a bathroom with twenty other families on their floor.

The cars were especially cool to see. The people had had to put their names on waiting lists to get one and often had to wait fifteen years before one was available. The cars were called Trabants and were only fifty-seven inches tall with just two cylinders.

That was one cold January and it stayed cold for a long time. Even Germany's six-week summer was cool by my standards. I didn't mind the temperatures so much as the overcast skies, however. Sometimes, the skies were bright, blue and clear, but too often; far too often, they were a pale, dull gray. And it rained a lot. Not the heavy thunderstorms I was used to, the kind that came down hard and then moved away, but rather the drizzling kind that stayed and just kept everything damp.

I found my favorite shopping spots and would jump on the bus just to get my favorite imported

❖

sandwich, a gyro, which was made with lamb, with pommes frîtes (French fries) smothered in curried ketchup, and prepared out of a street cart.

I visited a few German restaurants but I was not a big fan of the menus which favored slabs of meat with heavy gravies. I did enjoy the side dishes, such as braised red cabbage, warm potato salad and herbed spaetzle (noodles). The best part of the experience was the communal dining. We'd share a table with many other families and always had great conversations while loud Bavarian folk music played in the background.

Antonio introduced me to a few people. One of them was the girl I suspected had been keeping my husband company while I was still in the States. Was this man actually showing off his conquest? And was she bold enough to be up in my house? I wanted to kick both of their asses. Instead I told her that I had just gotten out of jail for fighting. That was partly true: I had spent some time in jail during the time I was waiting for my orders to go to Germany. I'd run off a loading dock and when the officers ran my license, they discovered I had an outstanding speeding ticket. I spent a few hours in jail until Mom came to get me. I wanted to intimidate Antonio's friend and that's all I could think of.

She was a 17-year-old Turkish high school student and very thin with muscular shoulders like a gymnast. Many of my husband's friends dated high school girls. It reminded me of the crew I used to hang with back in the States. A few of my high school friends who couldn't get a boyfriend in school were sleeping around with married soldiers. All the wives knew it and I had been fooling myself to think that everyone else's husband was doing it but mine.

❖

How had my dreams gotten this deferred? How in the world had I ended up here? Just a few years ago, I was the one, out of all of my friends, who was being made fun of because I was a nerd and talked about going to college. Tettie used to ask me, "Who do you think you are? One of the Cosby kids?"

Well, I definitely was not a Cosby kid, but wait – didn't one of them marry a soldier? I was different from the people I hung around with, but they were the one's who accepted me. Antonio used to tell me his family referred to me as "that uppity nigga." They thought that because I spoke well, I thought I was better than they were. If that were true, then I would have never visited for three long weeks in their dilapidated, roach-infested doublewide. I put up with roaches crawling all over my two-month-old baby and me. I was insulted but used to the name calling by then.

I couldn't stop thinking that I was the one who needed the ass kicking. If I'd stayed in school, I would've graduated that year with my B.A. in psychology.

It wasn't long before Antonio's misbehavior not only started again but also escalated to an all-time high. Every Friday night I could expect him to get drunk. We would argue if I were in the mood. And sometimes, if I drank a little liquid courage, I would get in his face, knowing full well it would get physical. Antonio was a big boy then. He'd gone from drinking cheap beer and Cisco, better known as bum wine, to hard liquor, like vodka and whiskey. In a matter of months he'd graduated from shoving to slaps or grabbing my arm so tightly that my knees would buckle, and then to full-blown closed-fisted punches to my face.

❖

When I wasn't in the mood to fight, he would just finish his drink and when the clock struck ten, put his glass in the sink and leave, sometimes without saying a word. The clubs didn't close until six in the morning and Antonio never left a club before the house lights came on. He'd come home, sober up and do it again Saturday night.

I never talked to Antonio on the weekends because he was either out partying, asleep or hung over. While he was out, playing single party animal, I was at home not only nursing our new baby daughter, but my physical and emotional wounds as well. I'd only been married a year but during that time I had experienced more hell than I'd ever dreamed possible.

I couldn't stand leaving my apartment. I was afraid that I would run into one of my neighbors. All but one of them could barely make eye contact with me and never made conversation. They were as uncomfortable around me as I was around them because they could overhear much of the constant fighting in our apartment. Mary Alice, the one neighbor who would talk to me, had issues of her own. She'd gained 200 lbs. after giving birth and her husband refused to touch her. Those walls were paper-thin. I used to hear her crying and begging her husband to make love to her.

As much as I couldn't stand those high school girls, they became a part of our lives, friends even. When we went to bar-b-ques or house parties they were there. I got to know them pretty well. But as soon as the wives would come from the States, the girlfriends would drop out of the scene. It was a strange situation.

One of the wives, Karen, had just arrived from New Orleans when her husband threw her a party to

❖

introduce her to some of the other wives. She asked me if I'd seen her husband with any girls. She pressed me to confirm her suspicions.

"It wouldn't have been the first time he cheated on me," she said.

I supposed she hoped that comment would make me feel more comfortable about breaking the news to her. I asked her why it took her a year to get to Germany when it had only taken me a month. I hoped that she would get that hint because that's all I would give her. I wanted to tell her the truth but I didn't. I didn't like the idea of being involved in someone else's drama. I was overwhelmed with my own.

Antonio was in his element. He had his booze to help him come out of his shell and his boys to encourage his behavior. He was the loud, trash talking, cigar-smoking, always-with-a-drink-in-his-hand clown at the table. Every card game has to have at least one. I would just sit back and watch him make a complete fool of himself, glad his attention was on something else rather than on making a complete fool of me.

In the meantime, I had started taking classes again. I'd always loved being in school, whether it was debating in my Gender Roles class or writing term papers. I enjoyed everything about it. I could feel my blood pumping again and I got my zest back.

On July 17, 1993 at exactly 9:00 p.m., I lost any hope that my marriage would get better. We were invited to Jeron and Lisa's house for a cookout. They lived in the next apartment building over. I arrived at their place a couple of hours after Antonio because Jeron had a reputation of being a drunk and physically abusive to his wife and I didn't want to be

❖

around him. They were a young couple with a child around a year old as well, but that was all we had common. I tried making small talk but that chick couldn't hold a conversation. I was frustrated with her one- and two-word answers, so I gave up and watched TV for the rest of the evening.

At one point, they pressured me to eat a leftover piece of steak. I was a little wary because it hadn't been touched but instead of trusting my instincts, I thought Jeron was proud of the steak and wanted to impress me. I didn't want to offend him, so I ate a little piece.

After the cookout, we decided to go to the bowling alley across the street from our apartment. It was a change for us and it felt nice. Jeron and Antonio chugged beer after beer all night long. I watched Antonio closely. He would get this disturbed glossy stare when he'd had too much alcohol. If I saw that stare, then I knew there would be trouble and I would leave. But I didn't see any signs of rage in his eyes, so I relaxed. We had a lot of fun, laughing and competing against each other, gals against guys. I had a couple of beers myself and was feeling fine. We played for three hours straight and the gals lost every game. I was glad to be out with Antonio and not fighting for a change.

I thought Antonio and I would go home together, tuck our daughter into bed and enjoy the rest of the evening together. I'd had more fun that evening than I'd had in a long time and I allowed myself to forget the hell I'd been living.

It was no more than a seven-minute walk from the bowling alley to our front door. We were almost home, when Jeron stopped cold.

"Hey, man. You want to go to the club," he asked Antonio.

❖

My stomach twisted into a knot. Please, say no, I prayed.

But of course he didn't.

I grabbed Antonio's arm. "No! Please! Come home with me."

I looked him in the eye so he could see my pain. I don't know why I always tried to appeal to his emotions when he was drunk because it never worked. He attempted to look back at me but he was so wasted he couldn't find my eyes and looked right past me. Then, without expression or hesitation, he gave a nod, turned his back on his home and headed off in the opposite direction.

I was sick. I couldn't believe this was happening. It was one thing to humiliate me behind closed doors, and quite another to do it in front of people. I walked back to my apartment, defeated. Lisa mumbled something about "how typical it was for men" and how her husband always did that to her.

Now, I knew that her husband was whipping her ass every night. But instead of commiserating with her, I got pissed at her for thinking that she and I were going through the same thing. The more she spoke, the angrier I got. My face grew warmer and I filled with rage. I didn't like my life being exposed. I could deal with living my hell alone, but once Antonio invited others to see what was going on, I couldn't. She should have pretended nothing was wrong, just as I was.

I tuned her out and told myself that I wasn't a victim. I had options and could walk away from that man at any time. If he could just stay sober long enough, he would come to his senses.

Lisa continued rambling.

❖

He never raised his voice or even thought about disrespecting me unless the devil's brew was running through his veins. The problem was the only time he was sober was when he was at work. I was so angry that I clinched my teeth and pressed my lips tight trying to control myself.

Lisa kept talking. I wanted to take all my anger out on her. I was glad we got to her building first because I was about to lose it upside her head.

I put my daughter to bed, stretched out next to her, and fantasized about leaving him. I don't even know what time he got home, but I really didn't care.

The next day, I had bad stomach cramps. I was on the floor in the living room all day long, moaning and groaning. Antonio walked by me several times ignoring me. He sat on the couch with his head in his hand, nursing his headache. I was still angry with him and didn't want to talk to him, but I couldn't take the pain, so I told him that I needed help.

He just looked at me. Then he continued to watch TV for a couple of minutes. Finally, he asked me if I was "really in that much pain."

"I think I got food poisoning from last night."

That's when he told me: The steak that I'd eaten had fallen on the floor.

I didn't know what to think or feel. "Well, if you knew it was dirty, why did you let me eat it?"

He shrugged. "I didn't think it would make you sick."

And then, he giggled. He actually giggled.

I couldn't believe it. What had really happened to that steak? Did it only fall on the floor or had he stepped on it? He couldn't have cared less if I were dead or alive. He'd tampered with my food.

❖

Our relationship was never the same. I started sleeping on the couch and refused all physical contact with him.

❖

Track 5

He Gave Me the Strength to Leave You

It took him to make me leave you.
He didn't even know my name.
When he saw you doing dirt to me,
He cared just the same.
He looks into my eyes,
'Cause he wants me to know the truth,
But can't so he beats around the bush.
He finally gets up the nerve
To ask me why I stay
With a man who disrespects me each and every day.
If you don't leave for yourself,
Leave for your beautiful child.
She's the one you should be thinking of,

And protecting her sweet smile.

After the poisoning incident, I became a social recluse. My classes had ended. I could've left at anytime. But I pretended nothing was wrong and played the good little housewife.

I stayed in my cocoon for six months. Summer passed, autumn came and went. Then it was the dead of winter and the only thing I was doing was going grocery shopping and taking Kaiya to the doctor. I wasn't even participating in play dates with the other mothers. Our entire world was limited to the four walls of our apartment.

It was easy for me to stay in my cocoon. I had everything I needed on post. The PX, commissary, bank, entertainment, restaurants, and everything else necessary to meet my outer needs were nestled inside a protective fence. That was one of the conveniences of living on a military installation. Physically, we were in another country, but in terms of day-to-day life, it was as if we'd never left the States. When I first arrived, I loved venturing out, but I had lost my zest and a restricted life on the base was just fine.

My only release came from going to the gym four times a week. Although I went to the gym because I loved to work out, I also went because it kept me from having to look at Antonio's face. Every other moment was spent with Kaiya.

I kept up that routine for months, until my husband's battalion sponsored a New Year's Eve party. I desperately needed some adult conversation and a change of scenery. I was ready to leave 1993 behind. My back was chiseled from working out so much and I picked out a gown that would show it off. I found a nice black, backless, floor-length, fitted dress that exposed the dimples on my lower back.

❖

I walked into the ballroom feeling good and with a rhythm to my step, singing the words to the song "Jump" in my head. I couldn't wait to see the Pointer Sisters perform. The ballroom was gorgeous. Black and silver balloons had been painstakingly draped across the ceiling and along banisters. The crystal chandelier that hung from the middle of the ceiling must have been fifteen feet across. Up the winding staircase, couples waited in line to take pictures. Everyone was dressed to impress; the soldiers wore their dress greens.

I searched the room for familiar faces and spotted a couple of free seats at a table with a few people I knew. Antonio went to join a few of his friends and I walked over to save our seats. The moment I sat down I felt a strange thickness in the air. These same people, with whom I'd hung out before, were acting as though they didn't know me. When I spoke, no one acknowledged me. They all ignored me. A couple of them even turned their backs to me.

I felt so uncomfortable that I got up to mingle. I spotted my friend Roula, who was from Beirut. I used to love talking to her because she reminded me of the old days back on the block in St. Louis. She'd left the danger of Beirut, immigrated to Germany seeking a better life, and married a soldier in Antonio's platoon. When someone upset her, she would throw her hands up and yell with a heavy accent, "You don't want to mess with me! I'm from Beirut!" the same way they did back home when they defended their turf. We got drinks from the bar and stood in line to get our picture taken together. We returned to our seats once they announced that the Pointer Sisters would perform in five minutes.

❖

Antonio was still gone and I searched the room for him. When I spotted him, he was in what seemed to be an intense conversation and looked unhappy. People glanced my way. Antonio walked over to our table and leaned over me, as if to say to his boys, 'Not only am I going to handle this, but I'm going to put my foot in her ass.'

Then he launched into me.

He accused me of having told Karen that her husband had been seeing another woman, one of those high school girls I mentioned earlier. Someone had written Karen a letter that included everything from the girl's name and age, to her phone number and address. His boy's convinced Antonio that I'd done it. Nothing I said could convince him otherwise. It hurt, but didn't surprise me, that he would take someone else's word over mine. He was never comfortable with being confronted by his peers. He needed his friends' approval more than mine.

His eyes were fixed and piercing. He began to get louder, so I got up and walked toward the door before we attracted too much attention. I hated being humiliated in public.

He followed me out and we walked to the car, arguing back and forth. Snow and ice had settled on the edges of the sidewalk. I was scared that I would break my ankle walking in those heels. He kept pushing me and I kept yelling at him to stop, but he wouldn't listen. When Antonio got angry with me, he made it his mission to inflict pain. He would let rage consume him.

Some might say that it would've made sense for me to have stayed at the party, where somebody might have intervened, but by then the effects of long-term terror controlled me. I thought that if no one saw the

❖

abuse, I could pretend it didn't exist. I had also known too many times where people wouldn't help. They stared, pointed, and laughed but did not step forward. I had reached a point at which I didn't think anyone really cared what happened to me. I was simply ashamed, embarrassed, and terrified of further humiliation.

Once we were in the car, he drew back and punched me in the face. The blow was so hard that it broke my glasses. It would leave me with a bruise across my left cheek and a cut across my eye. I was stunned. All I could do was hold my face and pray that he wouldn't hit me again.

During the car ride home, I felt an overwhelming rush of anger and resentment. I found the fighter I'd once been. As soon as we crossed the threshold of our apartment, it was on. We began throwing blows like two men. I picked up the phone and threw it at his head, but missed. He grabbed hold of my throat and choked me so hard that my lips turned numb. I remembered then why I'd stopped fighting him. My survival instincts kicked in and I pretended to pass out, but as soon as he let go and started to walk away I gathered all of my strength and kicked him as hard as I could. His legs buckled and he hit the floor hard. He landed on his knees and I kicked him again. He took a few moments to get himself together. I thought about running out of the apartment but was paralyzed with fear. When he started to get up, I jumped on him, closed my eyes and swung wildly with everything I had.

That was the last memory I had of that fight. The next day I woke up in the fetal position on the living room floor, battered and bruised. Before I even opened my eyes, I played it all back in my head. I wept

❖

because I realized how blessed I was to have survived that fight.

We spoke only when necessary after that; we simply shared a space. I cooked, I cleaned, and he played. I spent most of my time remembering my dreams. I had wanted to save all the bruised and battered souls of the world. Now, I had become one of them and needed someone to save me.

As long as I could stay out of Antonio's way, he didn't bother me. I yearned to go home, but couldn't find the nerve to ask Mom to take in Kaiya and me. I didn't want to feel like a failure again. I had to get myself out of that situation without depending on anyone else. I didn't know how I was going to do it but I knew I had to.

In June of 1994, a year and a half after my arrival in Germany, Antonio mentioned that we were moving to Mannheim because the Berlin army post was going to be closed in the early spring of '95. We were to leave in August, a week after my twenty-fourth birthday and two weeks before Kaiya would turn two. I wondered how we would throw her a birthday party when we wouldn't know anyone in Mannheim.

Antonio was good to Kaiya and he loved to dote on her. He had thrown a big party when she turned one. He organized everything. We didn't know many couples with small children so he had a grownup party in her honor. There were cases of beer cooling in the fridge, slabs of ribs on the grill, and two or three card tables set up for Spades games. She had a Barbie theme. The house was decorated with pink streamers and balloons. Kaiya sat at the head of the table with a two-foot-high Barbie cake that towered over her.

❖

Twenty grown men and women cheered her on as she blew out her tiny candle.

As soon as we arrived in Mannheim, I made a conscious effort to be among the living. I looked for a job and got to know my neighbors. They were very different from the ones in Berlin. They were a lot younger and really wild.

The wife across the hall was nineteen and everyone called her Tex-Mex. She had a boyfriend on the side and was contemplating leaving her husband for him.

The neighbor above us, Gloria, at 5'2", beat her 6'4" 230 lb. husband if he gave her any lip at all. He would lock himself in the bathroom, crying and begging for mercy, while she yelled through the door at all times of night. She found a letter he wrote to his cousin, suggesting the cousin join the military because of all the "fine ladies" to be met on field missions. She tried to beat him into being a good husband after that.

Tulip was the craziest of all. She got me a job at the convenience store with her. She was ghetto fabulous! She sported a peek-a-boo gold tooth in the front of her mouth and wore a wig she'd obviously had styled at the neighborhood salon back in Kansas City. It was asymmetrical on the top and long in the back like the group Salt and Pepa used to wear back in the day. To change looks, she would turn the wig to the right or left, and she was so small that she wore a size zero. She had no kids, stayed drunk, smoked a lot of weed and partied all the time. I envied her because she was so carefree and happy. Her husband tried his best to tame her but he couldn't get her to calm down. When he threatened to leave, she laughed. Tulip might have been tiny, but she was a giant when it came to controlling her world.

❖

We all hung out at each other's apartments and laughed about our bizarre lives. I felt somewhat normal, knowing other people's lives were just as messed up as mine. I loved hearing stories like the one in which Tex-Mex's son lost a piece of ham in his nose and didn't discover it until a week later when she smelled it decaying. Tulip described her nightclub hookups and Gloria's strange idea that allowing her sons to learn to cook would somehow turn them gay. My friends tried to advise me on how to deal with my situation. They were convinced they had the answers. Some of the advice was good, but I wasn't ready to take it.

On my days off I spent a lot of time shopping and taking day trips to the Czech Republic, especially to Prague, the capital city, to buy crystal. I collected crystal bells. I had tiny ones that I could hold in the palm of my hand and large delicate ones that I didn't pick up again after I put them on display. In Poland, I walked for miles at flea markets, searching for unique bric-a-brac.

I traveled all over Germany, especially during the holidays, to visit the outdoor Christmas festivals. I drank mulled wine, deliciously warm and seasoned with cinnamon sticks and cloves to warm the insides in freezing weather.

Whenever I could, I took weekend trips. I often went alone and let Kaiya hang out with her dad but sometimes Tulip accompanied me to the Polish flea markets. Antonio never cared if I traveled. In fact, he preferred it. He enjoyed his time with Kaiya. He'd take her to the park, and they would lounge on the couch all day and watch movies.

I'd take trips to Paris, snap pictures under the Eiffel Tower, the Arc de Triomphe, at Notre Dame,

❖

and the Louvre, I walked the Champs-Elysées, climbed the stairs to Sacré Coeur, marveled at the architecture and boated down the Seine. The beauty of Paris was a wonderful antidote, but only a temporary one, to the misery of my life in Mannheim.

Meanwhile, Antonio never got home before nine o'clock at night, and he was always drunk. He'd been riding his bike to and from work for about a month and a half. I suspected he had gotten in trouble for drinking and driving but I didn't dare ask. I pretended not to even notice. After seven months of no intimacy, he asked me why I wouldn't have sex with him. I looked him straight in the eyes and told him that I didn't have sex with men I didn't like.

In September, about nine months after being in Mannheim, I left the convenience store and started working evenings at Provisions, a new restaurant as a hostess/manager. The restaurant was great. It had themed rooms. There was the blues room where pictures of legendary blues artists like B.B. King and Billy Holiday, W.C. Handy and Bessie Smith were painted on the walls. The main dining room was called "Where Rock and Roll Meets Rhythm and Blues," and it was decorated with life-sized pictures of musicians, such as Michael Jackson, Madonna and Bruce Springsteen. Downstairs was a pub-style restaurant. Great music from the different genres played throughout the restaurant. After the reclusion of Berlin, I loved to socialize and was going to get paid to do it.

Before I started my new job, Antonio decided to take a weekend trip down to Berlin with a couple of his buddies. He'd been bragging about the nightlife down there since we moved, but I'm sure it was his girlfriend he really missed.

❖

When Antonio got back, he couldn't wait to tell me how he'd met another girl and spent the night with her and that she wanted him to go back the next weekend. Antonio made it his mission to get me to leave Germany so he could have a life without me in it. We had argued the week before and he told me he was going to do whatever he could to get me to leave. He didn't realize how numb I was to him or his words. He couldn't hurt me anymore.

My job was going well and I was finally happy. Antonio wasn't though. I dropped Kaiya at the babysitter's house at 4:00 p.m. Since I wasn't home in the evenings he had to go home right after work at 5:00 p.m. instead of his normal 9:00 p.m. to pick her up. Sometimes, he brought the parties to our house. I went weeks without seeing Antonio's face because I came home after he'd gone to bed, and he left in the morning before I woke up. It was easy to do with the two of us sleeping separately. I was at work when he was home and vice versa.

A regular at the restaurant had taken an interest in me. Craig was a half-white, half-Puerto Rican from Boston who thought he was a hip-hop artist from New York. He wore his jeans low and always sported a cap twisted to the side. He came in every Friday with his crew. He was too cool to speak and nodded instead, while throwing me his signature grin. He would watch me the entire night. I was flattered but pretended not to notice.

Sometimes the restaurant staff would go to a club after work. I wanted to go but was too scared to do so. If Antonio found out, I didn't know how he would react and I didn't want to find out.

For months, my co-workers pressured me to go with them. One night, I decided I could go for a couple

❖

of dances and get back before Antonio found out. He had to be at work at 5:30 a.m., so he was usually knocked out when I got home. I was sure I could get away with staying out late because I had been sleeping on the couch for more than a year.

It had been almost four years since I was on a dance floor and I had to work to get my groove back. I looked around, trying to pick up the latest moves but I felt so out of place. Finally, I walked off the floor to get a drink. Maybe, it would help me to relax. After my third drink, I was back on the dance floor, doing my thing. By that time, I didn't care if I looked funny or not.

I looked up and who did I see staring at me but Craig. I gestured for him to join me. He pretended not to know I was pointing at him, so I pointed again and then pointed down at my feet in a more demanding way, as if to say, "Front and center, soldier."

He and his friends laughed. Then he walked over with his shy, cool stroll and danced me right off the floor. He threw it this way and that and I couldn't keep up. I grabbed his arms to make him stop. I told him to slow down because he was hurting me. Finally, I saw him smile a real smile.

The DJ slowed the music down and all I heard was Guy, my favorite R&B group, playing "Piece of My Love," a song about secret lovers. The evening was beginning to resemble a cheesy love story. I wanted to walk away, but didn't. He started grinding on my leg as though he knew me. Everything he did was exaggerated.

He put his mouth next to my ear and I expected the regular boy meets girl questions like, "What's your name?" or "You gotta man?" But he asked neither.

❖

Instead he wanted to know why I let Antonio treat me the way he did.

I drew back, surprised.

"I know your husband," he said. He told me that he always saw Antonio at the barracks with different girls and that he'd seen him put his hands on me at the company cookout.

How long had Craig known me? Had he lived in Berlin as well? Because that's where Antonio used to really act a fool.

The questions swirled through my mind, but I never got a chance to ask them. Before I could say anything I felt a tap on my shoulder.

It was a stranger. "Antonio wants you," he said. "Outside. In the parking lot."

I was stunned. How did Antonio know where I was? My heart drummed in my chest. Had I been set up? I glanced at Craig for an explanation. He shrugged. He didn't know anything.

Well, I definitely was not going out there so Antonio could haul me away and beat the crap out of me again. This time I stayed in public where there would be witnesses. He was going to have to come in and get me.

And that's exactly what he did.

Craig glanced up, past my shoulder, and tensed. I didn't even have a chance to turn around before a strong hand gripped my neck and dragged me through the club. I grabbed Antonio's arm, broke away, and took off, running through the crowd. We had attracted a lot of attention, so by the time Antonio caught up to me, three huge security guards were there to pull him off of me and escort him out of the club. He yelled for them to let him go and that I was

❖

his wife – as though my being his wife gave him the right to drag me out of a club by my clothes.

His eyes were full of blind rage – and a determination to get me. Why was he there? More importantly, where was our daughter? Then I realized it was Friday and he didn't have to go to work the next day. He'd probably been at home waiting for me so he could go out. His friends must have called him and told him I was there.

The stranger returned. "Antonio says he wants you to go outside and he's not leaving till you do."

I shook my head, no.

The guy went out to deliver the message, then returned and asked for the house key and the car key. I gave up the house key but held on to the car key. No way in hell was I going to be stranded out there without my car.

Whoever this guy was, he didn't come back with any more demands. I stayed in the club until it closed, hoping that Antonio had given up and gone home. Then I went to the babysitter's house and, low and behold, there was our daughter asleep on her pallet.

The sitter told me that Antonio had dropped Kaiya off at about a half hour past midnight. That would've been about thirty minutes after I'd gotten to the club. I told her what happened and she invited me to spend the night.

The next day, I called the house but Antonio wouldn't answer the phone. I was sure he was home because I drove by and saw his car in the parking lot. I knocked for about twenty minutes but he wouldn't let us in. So Kaiya and I had to spend another night at the sitter's.

❖

I spent all day thinking about what Craig said, about how Antonio lived another life at the barracks with his girlfriends. I was getting angrier and angrier, not because of his philandering, but because Kaiya and I were stranded, with no clean clothes or toothbrushes. It was humiliating to have to sit in someone else's house, the dirty laundry of our marriage hung out for her to see.

She convinced me to press charges and agreed to watch Kaiya while I went to the MP station. Antonio's commanding officer showed up right after I got there and tried to talk me out of pressing charges. I didn't even get a chance to complete the paperwork. Nothing felt real at that point. It was as if I'd fallen into an episode of the "Twilight Zone." I wanted to know where the cameras were.

I told the MPs and the C.O. everything about how I was threatened and attacked at the club. I told them how my keys had been taken away and Antonio had locked us out of our apartment for two days. The C.O. pressured me not to press charges. He said Antonio could lose everything, his career, his pension, and his GI bill. He leaned forward, took my hands as if he really cared, and promised me that he would take care of everything. The MPs assured me they would pursue charges without me. The fact that an incident occurred was all they needed, and that made me feel better about dropping them. I don't know if the charges were pursued or not. I never heard anything about it again.

I left there with my head hung low and tail tucked tightly between my legs. I tried to believe the assurances I'd been given. I told myself that since the C.O. would call Antonio, it was safe to go home.

But life got worse after that.

The night I returned, Antonio called at 10:00 p.m. to ask if there was any dinner left. When I said I hadn't cooked anything, he told me to go out and get something for him. I flat out refused. Kaiya was sleeping and I wasn't going to wake her up just to fetch his supper. He could get something himself. He told me he was on his bike and that he couldn't carry anything. He was angry, talking through clenched teeth. What would he do once he got home? He asked me if I had a man in the house. Whatever he was on was making him extremely paranoid.

When he got home, I pretended to be asleep and hoped he would just go to bed. Instead, he stood over me. When I wouldn't open my eyes, he shouted my name until I did.

His eyes burned with hatred. I begged him not to hurt me. I just knew I was going to have to fight for my life. He leaned over me, a tight fist raised, ready to bash my head in. He liked hitting me anywhere above my neck. He didn't try to hide his abuse. My scars were like badges of honor to him. He hovered over me for about three minutes before he finally walked away.

He came back about thirty minutes later and lay on top of me. He grabbed my breasts hard and pressed his face into mine. He held my arms above my head with one hand while pulling my pajama bottoms down with the other. His hot, liquored breath stung my nose and lingered in my throat. I yelled for him to get off of me, but he ignored me. We tussled for about five minutes before he completely overtook me. My body went limp, unable to fight back anymore.

The longer he violated me, the more outraged I became. I put my mouth as close to his ear as I could and said, "If you're determined to do this, you better

❖

be ready to accept the consequences. I won't drop the charges this time."

He immediately stopped, but then he grabbed a handful of my hair. I could feel him contemplating his next move. His body tensed and jerked as if he were trying to hold back tears. He grabbed my hair tighter and pulled even harder before he finally let me go.

I lay awake all that night, worrying. What could I use to protect myself if he came back again? I reflected on the real reason that I was still in Germany, living like a trapped animal, fearing for my life: I was too embarrassed to return home with a failed marriage and have to admit that I'd made a mistake. Despite all the punches, shoves, and disrespectful words that man had heaped on me, I'd left college for him. I didn't want to go home and end up like the women in my family. Every one of them is a single mother whose spirit was sucked dry while they worked themselves to the bone to take care of their children alone. I didn't want to be like them, having to do it all and do it alone.

Antonio's tour of duty was up in December of 1995. He was twenty-five, I was twenty-four and Kaiya had turned three. Mom came to visit for Thanksgiving and Christmas. During those six weeks, she witnessed Antonio's rage up close and ugly. He would come home at six in the morning and stand over me. While Mom lay next to me, he would call me a whore and a slut and tell me that he'd seen my "boyfriend" with another girl. Despite Antonio's repeated infidelity, he was still furious over having seen me that one time in another man's company. This was the first time Mom had any indication my marriage was in trouble. I wanted her help but didn't know how to ask for it. Her

❖

heart was heavy; she knew I was in trouble but in her wisdom she knew I had to work it out on my own.

Craig still stopped by the restaurant every Friday to check on me and talk. He encouraged me to leave Antonio. He reminded me that I deserved much better treatment. I agreed but I didn't know how to leave or where to go.

"It's killing me to see how Antonio is hurting you," Craig said. "I wish I could help."

For a moment, I fantasized about him taking me away, rescuing me. Then he told me that his unit was to be deployed to fight in the Gulf War.

"We're supposed to leave in two weeks."

I was so sad and surprised, I couldn't answer.

"Ayo," he said, "I'm telling you, you've got to get out. If you won't do it for yourself, then do it for Kaiya."

That last comment rang loud in my ears. I hadn't even thought about how our fighting must have been affecting our daughter. Craig was right. I couldn't have her around all that ugliness anymore.

By then, Antonio had gotten so paranoid that if he couldn't find me in the restaurant's dining room, then he would go around back and peer through the kitchen windows. The entire staff was in jitters. For their sake as well as mine, I thought it would be safer to quit my job.

One evening, Kaiya, Mom and I went out to enjoy the Christmas festival in downtown Mannheim. We returned home to find Antonio waiting outside for us. Later, he'd say he'd locked himself out of the house, but, as soon as we got out of the car, he rushed me and accused my mother of helping me cheat on him. I was so stunned I couldn't respond. I walked past him and let myself in the house. I kept my eyes

❖

straight ahead, refusing to make eye contact or dispute anything because I didn't want him to get angrier. Once inside, however, I told him that I wasn't going to Ft. Drum with him.

He laughed. "And just where do you think you're going then?"

I couldn't do anything except shrug because I really didn't know.

"You'll never leave me," he said. "You need me. You know you can't make it on your own. You never could."

I had an uneasy feeling in the pit of my stomach but there was no turning back. I was determined to prove him wrong.

The morning Antonio left for the States he threw a tantrum because he couldn't find the 35mm camera we received while attending a time-share seminar. Antonio took everything electronic. He left me with the furniture: a couch, two chairs and a wall unit. If it plugged into a wall he was going to take it: the televisions, stereo equipment, and the computer and, if he could find it, our camera, too.

Ah, but could he find it? It was the one thing of value I kept because it was easy to hide. He ranted and raved all morning about that camera. I was scared but denied knowing where it was.

His ride came, but he wouldn't leave. Mom sat on the couch while our daughter and his friend stood inside the door, watching him carry on about the camera. He got in my face and tried to intimidate me but I didn't flinch. I continued not to acknowledge his threats. I knew he wanted to hit me because he was in that stance again. I knew he pictured himself putting me on the floor because I was picturing it too.

❖

"Hey," his friend said, "we got to get going or we're going to miss the flight."

Antonio hesitated, torn between his need to go and his hatred of me.

I was standing by the stove. As I looked down at my pot of grits, I had a Mary Woodson moment and thought that if he put his hands on me he would have had an Al Green moment. My heart was hammering in my chest.

I took the spoon out of the pot and held it down by my side. He backed off when he saw that. I looked him directly in the eye. He worked his jaw and for a moment, I thought he'd charge, but after a few seconds, he gave a grunt of disgust, grabbed up his duffle bag and walked out, slamming the door. He didn't even say good-bye to Kaiya.

An overwhelming sense of relief washed over me. It was December 1995 and a turning point. I knew that Antonio would never threaten or hurt me again.

❖

Track 6

Try Again

It's been five years since I let a man
Woo me in an attempt to take my hand.
It didn't take much.
In fact, I approached him.
Guess I'm ready to try it again.
Got my head right and feeling good.
Maybe this one will treat me the way he should.
It's been five years since I let a man
Touch me anywhere but on my hand.
On my neck, my hips or the small of my back.
It's nice to feel this again
And allow myself to be totally free,
To love you unconditionally.

We left Germany one week later. Antonio had given

me only ninety dollars. It would have been enough, but the military wouldn't fly us back to Missouri, so I had to take a bus from Atlanta to Rolla, Missouri, where Mom now lived. Rolla was about thirty minutes west of Waynesville. It was just as small as Waynesville, but it was a college town with a Walmart, so it didn't feel as rural. Kaiya and I walked roughly seven blocks from the airport to the bus station. I struggled with two large bags while Kaiya walked with her baby doll. The bus tickets for both of us totaled ninety-one dollars, one dollar more than we had. The agent must've seen something in my eyes because she reached into her pocket and added her dollar to my bill. That was a kindness I'll always remember.

Kaiya hadn't eaten in more than twenty-four hours. She was only 3, but she never cried or complained once. She was a strong kid and her strength kept me strong.

My mother met us at the bus stop in Rolla and took us straight to an IHOP. It was a bittersweet reunion. It was nice to have finally left such a terrible situation, but having once left home, it was hard to go back. The fear of not knowing what I was going to do and the loss of my husband was overwhelming. Over the next months, I would cry often, but never waver in my decision. Leaving him was the best move for my child and me. Some days were so hard that I had to call my older sister for an ear to listen and to hear caring words.

In August, Mom bought me a car, I enrolled Kaiya in daycare and I enrolled in Columbia College, where I excelled. Soon after, I got a job at a group home for adolescent girls and boys and a job at a shelter for abused women and children. I went to school during the day, worked at the shelter from 11 p.m. to 7 a.m. Monday to Friday and worked at the group home from midnight Friday to 8 a.m. Monday morning. I couldn't have done it without Mom's help. She watched Kaiya while I took classes in the evening.

Some of the kids at the adolescent home were tough. There was the 17-year-old girl who'd broken her cousin's back for calling her a bitch. There was the boy who was in for being a sex offender.. He was eleven years old and only weighed about eighty pounds. Most of the kids had been placed in the shelter because they had irresponsible parents.

Unfortunately, my experience at the shelter made me want to change my career. The work was emotionally very trying. I was so young myself and still in a lot of pain from my own abusive situation. I worked hard with the women to give them a sense of empowerment and the courage to leave their abusive partners. It was way too difficult for me to handle seeing them return to their abusers time and time again.

Overall, we had a success rate of only five percent. These women faced huge hurdles, including the justice system itself. It was a small town with a small town mentality, so even the judges believed that a man had a right to rule his house in whatever way he wanted, even if that meant knocking his wife's teeth out to keep her quiet. The women's stories and the judicial injustices they suffered infuriated and frustrated me. I couldn't handle their issues and deal with my healing as well.

Mom's house soon became too crowded for us. My youngest sister, Shani, was at home as well and thirty weeks pregnant with her first son, Tariq, so I got my own apartment. Shani was twenty-two and pregnant by her high school sweetheart of nine years.

❖

The wedding date was set, but three weeks before the baby was due they called it off. She couldn't break the family cycle either and would give birth to another fatherless child.

It took another two years of working and studying, but I completed my B.A. in psychology and graduated with honors in May of 1997.

I had not seen or spoken to my father since I left St. Louis when I was fifteen, but I invited him and his wife to my graduation. I didn't know him very well, but I wanted to. A dad is a dad is a dad, and one of the things that dads do is attend their child's graduation. So stranger or not, he got an invite. It made perfect sense to me.

Mom and my older sister, Naja, surprised me with a weekend trip to Jamaica for graduation. Naja went with me and Mom watched Kaiya. I appreciated the trip but felt that the timing was bad. Without school, work, and my child to keep my mind occupied, I had too much time to get lost in my misery. It didn't matter that a beautiful ocean, coconut trees, and an all-you-can-eat buffet surrounded me. I was still trying to shake the last five years of my life.

It was hard to relax on the beach and not have flashbacks of being punched in the face or called some horrible name. I couldn't find joy in anything. Signs of my anxiety and anger crept into every situation.

I moped around and lost my temper several times. Even the sailboat guides laughter set me off. They were having a good time and their laughter pissed me off. Naja tried her best to make me happy but I needed professional help. My misery was too much for her and just about ruined the weekend.

I needed to move out of that small town. Naja invited me to move to Orlando, where she lived at the

❖

time because she thought I might have better job opportunities. I didn't think twice. I graduated in May, relocated in June, was employed by July and started my master's program in August. I decided to get my degree in Human Resources Development with an emphasis on training and development. I knew that I could still change lives through education.

Shortly after Antonio and I split up, he'd had another daughter. The mother was a married female soldier who already had six other children. Her family hated him. The woman was so distraught that she ended up in a mental ward. By the time I found out about her it was 1998 and the baby was three years old. I only learned about it because the military issued me a summons to appear at his court-martial. Eventually, it would discharge him for having an adulterous affair. That was the end of his military career.

Technically, I was still married. My marital status didn't bother me because I had no intention of meeting anyone. Professional success was all I cared about. I'd gone back to school and received my bachelor's and master's degrees in four years. I had accomplished more by myself than I was ever able to do with him.

Orlando was great. It was sunny and hot, just the way I liked it. It was a bit humid but I'd take humidity over snow any day. There were the lovely palm trees that lined the beautifully manicured streets. Everyone had a swimming pool. Even the most run-down apartment complexes had pools. My salary was low, but so was the cost of living.

I met Regina at work. We'd moved to Orlando in the same month and begun our jobs the same day. She was a feisty, self proclaimed "Neuro-Rican." She

❖

was loud and proud. I, on the other hand, was calm and reserved and awed by her wild and spontaneous personality. She had more attitude in one of her baby toes than I had in my whole body. We both had tragic stories. The main difference was that I was running from mine and she was running toward hers. She'd just found her children, Elaine and Vladimir, ages fifteen and sixteen, respectively. They'd been kidnapped and taken to Mexico as toddlers by her ex-husband, who was twenty years her senior. Some family members had tipped her that the children were in Florida. Without much thought she and her new husband, Carlos, along with her 8-year-old son, Gabrielle, had packed up their lives and moved to be close to them.

It was around this time that I also met Brandon. He came to open a clogged drain in my apartment. He was gorgeous in those days. I'd seen him in the weight room a few times obsessively working his abs and arms, doing two hundred sit-ups and push-ups every night. He was well put together. His hair was cut short and his goatee neatly trimmed. He was kind of short, at 5 feet 6 inches, but he looked just like that beautiful soap opera star Shamar Moore.

I was instantly attracted to him, but we hit it off only as friends. He couldn't stop talking about his ex-girlfriend who was twenty years older. I should have known it wouldn't have worked between us. Obviously, he liked significantly older women and I was only two years older than he was.

He would come over with a six-pack of Corona, a bottle of tequila for me, and a dime bag for himself. He was a bigger pothead than Tulip. We would talk all night long, staying up until 5 a.m. I became his counselor and enjoyed the company. We shared

❖

relationship horror stories. I did get tired of him only talking about this woman who never appreciated him, though. I wanted to say, "Get over her," but I knew better than anyone that you can't rush the healing process.

We kept this routine on and off for a couple of months. I considered him a really good friend. He would help me out with my car and lend me money or whatever else I needed and I would do the same for him. Then one day, I came home with Kaiya, checked the voicemail and found a message from a strange woman. She'd cussed me out, told me to stay away from her man. Brandon called later that evening. Crying, he said he was sorry but he wouldn't be able to see me again. I figured he was back with his girlfriend. I knew he was still in love with her. But I was confused about why he was crying.

Two weeks later he showed up at my door with a six-pack like nothing had ever happened and we picked up right where we left off. He and his girlfriend had broken up for good that time. Apparently, there was a big commotion and she'd even spent a night in jail for hitting him. They lived only a few apartment buildings down from mine. I don't know how I missed that action.

After about a month of relative normalcy he called again to say that he was leaving town and that he would never see me or talk to me again. He was crying again and this time he scared me. His undertone sounded suicidal. He wouldn't tell me what was wrong so I talked to him the same way I would when he was at my house crying about his ex-girlfriend.

"No matter what you're going through, I'll be there for you," I said.

❖

When we hung up, I didn't expect to ever see him again. It was just as well. He brought too much drama. I wanted to keep my life drama-free and put him behind me. But a week later, there he was again, with a six-pack, tequila and a couple of joints. I looked at him and suddenly understood.

"Are you on medication?" I asked. There had been signs. I don't know how I didn't see them.

For the next couple of years, life was as normal as could be expected. I worked, went to graduate school in the evenings and took care of Kaiya as best I could. We were doing well. Regina watched Kaiya for me when I was in class. We hung out together all the time. I taught her how to drive and she taught me how to Salsa. We spent every holiday together. She loved to watch the sun set, so every once in a while her crazy tail would drag me on a two-and-a-half hour ride to Tampa to watch a 15-minute sunset over the water. Then she'd turn right back around and drive another two-and-a-half hours back home. I attended her son's soccer games and was there when Vladimir graduated from high school. I was also there to console her after she threw Carlos out of the house for having an affair.

In the summer of 1999, the year I completed grad school and, two years after moving to Orlando, Mom moved to Virginia. Shani chose to stay in Missouri. I got custody of Tariq because Shani found it too difficult to raise him on her own. He was two years old. I gladly agreed to take him until she could get herself together. Mom drove Tariq from Missouri to Florida and gave me her car.

That same summer, Antonio took leave to visit Kaiya. He was discharged from the military by then and moved to Texas with his older brother and started driving trucks. He bought groceries, footed the bill for

❖

a trip to Miami, and paid for me to get a tattoo. We had a good time. He even apologized for our torrid marriage. He said he'd hit me because he was afraid of losing me. He thought the solution was to control me and didn't know what else to do.

"You were my first. I was so in love and I couldn't handle it," he said.

We actually had fun together. For a fraction of a second I thought about how it would be if we got back together, but only for a fraction.

Antonio couldn't wait to show me a picture of one of his new girlfriends. Her name was Nichole. She was nineteen, from the Bahamas, and studying to be a nurse in the army.

He told me that it was nothing serious. He was looking for a sugar mamma to take care of him, he said, because he would be leaving the military soon. I reminded him that we were as young as she was when we met and that he shouldn't play with her feelings like that, especially if he wasn't ready to be serious. I urged him to let her go because it wasn't fair to her.

I felt bad for that girl. What was her story? She must have had some hidden childhood issues, was emotionally unstable like his last girlfriend or just plain stupid because no one with anything going for them would have had anything to do with Antonio. I did notice that she looked a bit older than her nineteen years and that she had sad eyes.

His ego never let him forget that I refused to have sex with him for the last year and a half of our three-year marriage. The only thing he remembered was that I said he was horrible in bed. Not realizing that I couldn't enjoy sex with someone I couldn't stand, he pressured me about showing me how good he was since he had been getting "a lot of practice." All week I refused his offers. He wouldn't let it go and that made me very curious. I wanted to see if it was true and I let him show me. I still regret it. Afterward, he was so cocky. He felt like "The Man." And no, it wasn't any better than I remembered. But then again, I still couldn't stand him.

That August, a community center in Pine Hills offered me a job as a counselor. Pine Hills was one of the roughest areas in Orlando. Its residents referred to it affectionately as Crime Hills. The familiar sounds of fellas playing bones and talking smack, the rattling from old cars passing by, and the laughing of ladies gossiping while perched on a stoop of big mama's house, reminded me of St. Louis.

I worked with 10- and 11-year-olds and their families. It was exactly what I wanted to do: work with inner city kids who needed guidance. In many cases, I was older than their mothers. I was only twenty-eight, which means they were having their children in their mid-teens. Some of the kids referred to me as "Mamma Ayo." It felt good to make a difference in their lives.

The center was in an old building. It was going through a major electrical renovation to get it up to code, so there were construction crews all over. One day, I was in a meeting in my office when I heard a knock at the door. An electrician wanted to get to the utility closet. When he saw that I was in a meeting, he ducked back out, saying he would return later.

I served in a community that was mostly Haitian, Jamaican, and African-American, and I lived in a Puerto Rican neighborhood. So, I'd learned to recognize specific accents. However, I didn't recognize his.

He came back a few hours later when he was sure I had no clients. He reminded me that he was there to look at the fuse box.

"Oh," I said, "I thought you came back to see me."

I don't know where that came from, but I was flirting with that man. He replied with a bashful grin. It had been almost five years since I left my husband. I'd chosen not to date during that time because I wanted to make sure my head was right. I didn't want to make the same mistake I'd made with Antonio.

The electrician's name was Felix and he was from Tobago. He was 6'4", completely bald and without facial hair. He was also very polite. When I left work that evening, I saw Felix and one of his co-workers waiting at a bus stop. I made a U-turn right in the middle of Hiawassee Road and offered them a ride. As soon as I got home, I jumped online to find out about Tobago.

The next thing I knew I was dating again. For the next year, Felix and I spent time together. It wasn't great but it was nowhere near as troublesome as what I'd experienced with Antonio. I enjoyed our low-key relationship. He was thirty-seven and I was twenty-nine. Because he was older, I thought I was dating a mature man. If he'd been younger, I would've dumped him much sooner because he was kind of boring. I was so naïve; I thought mature meant boring. Nothing worked on him. He had bad knees and high blood pressure, so our sex life was incredibly different from what I remembered with Antonio when he and I met. Antonio was adventurous and he had a lot of stamina. When Felix and I were intimate, it was always in one position and it never lasted more than half an hour, including foreplay.

❖

We had a routine. He came over at 9 p.m. every evening after my kids went to bed, and left every morning before they woke up. I didn't want my kids to meet anyone until I was sure it was going to last. We hung out on the weekends, and he took me to dances, took the kids and me to cookouts and introduced me to his friends. He had a nice circle of friends. They were older with no drama. They were all married and in what appeared to be solid long-term relationships. I felt really comfortable with them. I thought Felix and I were going to have a life together. My babysitter was the wife of an electrician that he worked with and she told me that he'd been referring to me as "the one."

In May 2000, ten months after I'd started working at the center, it lost a grant and I lost my job. I couldn't find another position to save my life. I signed up with headhunters and temp agencies, and applied at convenience stores but couldn't find anything. A headhunter advised me to dummy down my resume. She thought I wasn't getting calls because most of the supervisors she worked with were less educated than I was. I couldn't believe that I'd lost a job making only $27,000 a year and all of a sudden was overqualified.

I tried hard to keep my lights on, feed my kids, and not lose our apartment. I was trying equally as hard not to lose my mind. It was becoming increasingly difficult to maintain a household on unemployment. I was frustrated because neither Antonio nor my nephew's mother was paying child support on a regular basis. When Shani found out I'd lost my job, she did help me some and it kept me from losing my apartment, but in hard times "some help" isn't enough. Antonio was missing in action. After he left the military, the money I received from him left as

❖

well. I couldn't find him anywhere. Maybe he'd found his sugar mamma after all. I used to feel like the only person on the planet who had a deadbeat baby mamma and daddy.

The cupboard was bare and one by one my utilities were disconnected. I turned to alcohol to help me escape. Every time I found a $1.25, I ran down to 7-Eleven to buy a beer. That beer was cheap and the can was so huge that I could barely put my hands around it; it did the trick.

I realized that Felix wasn't the best under pressure either. I called Naja weekly to vent about my situation and how Felix didn't seem to care about what I was going through. He never offered to help. When my lights were cut off, Felix wouldn't answer his phone. For the most part I was strong and handled the pressure but every once in a while I would breakdown in front of him and he would give me some lame cheer up speech that would only depress me more. I felt like kicking him in his arthritic knees and yelling, "Shut up and just listen. No one asked you to speak. All I need is money to feed my kids. So just listen and lock the door on your way out."

I used to tell my best friend Regina everything – until I got tired of her telling me how stupid I was to allow men to take advantage of me. She couldn't stand Felix. She would tell me in her thick New York "Spanglish" that I needed to dump his ass if he didn't give me money, buy me groceries, or help me with my bills and that, since I was giving him sex, the least he could do was let me stay in his house. The only thing I ever said was, "I know Regina."

"My daddy used to tell me 'if you dance with a man and he doesn't buy you a drink afterwards, you don't give him a second one.' Didn't your daddy teach you anything? I mean dang, Ayo. You have to know when a man is full of trickery or feeding you a line of shigidy. What can you possibly be getting out of this?" Regina always created kid-friendly cuss words like shigidy when her son was around.

She'd ask me why I hadn't taken my ex to court for child support and say there was no reason I should be struggling that way. All I could say was, "I know Regina."

She was a hustler. She never wanted for anything. We only made $24,000 a year as telephone counselors, but she never struggled. Her boyfriends paid for everything, from packages of ground chuck to her rent. She always had a roommate, sometimes two. She would sleep on her couch in the living room to put money in her pocket. I thought she was the crazy one. Now, she owns her own home and I'm still struggling.

❖

Track 7

Made Whole Again

Who was I
Before you came into my life
And touched my pain?
When I tried to walk away,
You found a way to make me stay.
You said yes,
I said no,
You laid me down
And loved me slow.
At that moment,
I knew then
My life was now made whole again
Others may know
What I've been through.
Yet no one knows me
 As you do.

You can see my joy,
You can take my fear,
You can touch my soul,
And make heaven appear.
If my heart could speak,
You'd hear it say
I love you more
With each passing day.
All my dreams
Have now come true,
All made possible
Because of you.
Never again,
Will you be alone,
Because in my heart
You'll have a home.
Who was I
Before you came?
A woman in part
Made whole again.

My lease was up in September and I had to move from my apartment. I couldn't find anyone to buy my beautiful leather sectional and a treadmill so I ended up giving them away. Then I drove around, finding dumpsters to throw away the other big items, including the wall unit I'd bought in Germany, because I had no money to store them. Felix was nowhere to be found. I called Naja to vent about no one offering to help me. "Ayo, there are people who want to help, but you're going to have to ask." Too full of pride, I didn't call anyone except Brandon to help me get my TV down the stairs. He didn't arrive until

2:00 a.m., but at least he came and as soon as the TV was in my car he took off again.

I moved in with an ex-coworker, Francine, who had a few issues of her own. I rented one of her bedrooms and the kids and I crowded onto a single bed. Sometimes, the kids ended up sprawled across the floor. I never knew if they fell out or got out to have more room.

One morning I woke up late and had to rush to get my daughter to school on time. Tariq was three and not in school yet. He'd gone to Missouri to visit Shani for a couple of weeks. This was the first time he'd seen her since he'd come to live with me. I slept so much it felt like my bones had fused together and that morning was especially rough. It hurt to roll out of bed. I had just enough time to wash Kaiya and then jumped in the car, still wearing what I'd slept in: a flimsy brown t-shirt, red plaid pajama pants, and no underwear. As we ran toward the door, I slid into a pair of pink terrycloth house shoes.

In the middle of John Young Parkway, at the height of the morning rush hour traffic my old, beat up and just as depressed Toyota Corolla decided to end it all, right then and there. It just stopped moving. I sat through three lights, feeling overwhelmed and despairing. With the way my luck was going, I knew no Good Samaritan was going to help. I knew I would sit there until a cop showed up. Once he saw me and realized the condition of my car, he'd cart me off to the 33rd Street Jail, which was only about two blocks away. Not only was I driving a car that wasn't insured, I'd committed the far worse crime of "driving while ugly."

I heard two beats on the trunk and a man with a strong accent yelled for me to put the car in neutral.

❖

I was startled. It wasn't the cops after all; it was worse. The most beautiful man on the planet was at my bumper, crouched down, looking right at me through my driver's side window.

I put the car in neutral and steered toward a gas station as the car was pushed from behind. What had I done to deserve this new embarrassment? I hadn't brushed my teeth or washed my face and I could smell my armpits. I would've rather had the cops there.

Once the car was out of traffic, I sat there hoping he would just give me a wave and be on his way, but he didn't. After I got up the nerve to look up, I saw that he was standing directly at the driver's door. I got out of the car too mortified to look him in the eyes.

Once I did look up, I realized that three men helped push my car out of the road. One of them was big and burly, with hair about six inches long that stood up all over his head. The other two men were slight in stature. They were all very handsome, obviously laborers on their way to work. Their clothes were ripped and stained with paint.

I needn't have worried about looking them in the eyes; they sure weren't looking in mine. They were all staring at my T-shirt. It was as if they were having a staring contest with my nipples. How long would this game go on before one of us would break?

Finally, after what seemed like an eternity, one of them asked me what had happened. I told them that my car had committed suicide. They burst out in laughter. Then the big guy took control of the situation and asked me to lift "the bonnet." I had no idea what the bonnet was and was too embarrassed to

❖

ask. Obviously, it had something to do with the car, but what?

"The bonnet?" I repeated.

They chuckled at the look on my face.

"Pop the hood," one of them said.

"Oh," I said and did.

The big guy fiddled around under the hood a bit and then said, "You need oil. Got any money?"

I reached into the car and took out my last twenty dollars. I kept it in the ashtray. It was all I had until my next unemployment check. He pried it from my hand and went inside the gas station. Left outside, the other two men chatted me up.

We introduced ourselves. Still embarrassed, I tried to cover myself without being too obvious. The fellow who said his name was Carl did most of the talking and introduced Noel as well.

Noel was very cute and had a voice so sweet that his words blended into a song. It had a strange tone, as if he held his tongue in the back of his throat. His accent was the heaviest of the three. I assumed he had not been in the country long. I asked him where he was from and he serenaded me, "Kingston, Jamaica." His voice resonated right through me. His brow was pronounced. His eyes were very serious and direct. It was as if he were trying figure out what my story was without asking. Damn, he was beautiful and I was standing out there looking a hot mess.

He asked me about the tattoo on my right shoulder. I told him that it was a Chinese character that meant "angel." He asked me how I knew that and then he and Carl started laughing again. The teasing further upset me. They didn't know me and besides, didn't they have any compassion for a girl who had just suffered the terrible loss of her car? Couldn't they

❖

see my condition? I didn't say anything else about the tattoo.

Then the questions really began. Carl asked me where my man was. I just shrugged and tried not to show my irritation. The questions continued for as long as it took for the big guy, who turned out to be Noel's big brother, Thomas, to return with two quarts of oil. He kept my change. I was desperate to have it back, but I was too intimidated to ask. He put the oil in the tank, tinkered around a bit and hooked our batteries up to give my car a jump.

"Your starter is bad," he said and then ordered me to start the car and press the gas.

I felt a wave of relief as my car came back to life. The men told me to let it run for about fifteen minutes before I turned it off. They gathered their belongings and Carl gave me his number and told me to call later that evening. He would take another look at the car if it were still giving me trouble.

They left, just as quickly as they came. As soon as they pulled out of the parking lot, my car took its last and final breath. I tried to flag them down but they didn't look back. Off they went and I was left sitting again, with my daughter in the back seat, in a dead car, looking a mess, and now without a dime to my name.

I grabbed Kaiya, locked up the car, and began the long walk home. Even though it was about 8:45 in the morning that Florida sun was beating down on us hard. My armpits were screaming back at me by then. Luckily, Francine spotted us and took my daughter to school.

That afternoon, I called Felix to pick my daughter up from school. When I told him what happened he showed absolutely no concern. Felix

❖

rarely showed much emotion though. I looked for a sign in his eyes that he felt bad for me or wished he could've been there for me. I told him how strangers had helped me and given me their number to call if the car continued to give me trouble. I thought he would be a little concerned about the three strange men or at least with the number I got. I just knew the next words out of his mouth would be, "No! I, Akhenaton! You, Nefertiti! Only I shall touch the chariot of my queen."

Instead, he just sat there listening to the new Calypso CD he'd downloaded from the Internet the night before. He didn't even offer to help get my car back home. Oh, he did ask me what I'd done with my wall unit.

After a year and a half of dating, he and I had problems. It forced me to see him for who he really was and what I really was to him. My fragile state kept me from leaving him because I didn't have anyone else. By then, a look of irritation had replaced his once constant grin. My constant need had become a burden.

When he dropped us off at the house he asked me to wait. He got out and I followed him to the trunk. I thought he was going to give me money, a long comforting hug, something that showed he cared. Instead, he opened the trunk and pulled out a basket of dirty laundry.

This was the first time Felix had been to the United States. Tobago is only twenty-five miles long and he knew just about everyone in his tiny community. I called him Tricky, because when I first met him, his face was set in a grin, as if he knew something I didn't, like he'd just told a joke and was waiting for me to get the punch line. Now I realized

❖

that the joke was on me. He was grinning because he thought I was a sucker and would do anything he asked.

He was right.

I stood in the middle of the street, staring at the basket of clothes. I didn't even have the energy to give him the "are you crazy" look. You know the one where you step back on one leg, cock your head to the side, while your mouth is slightly open with one side of your top lip curled up? The only energy I could muster was to extend my arms. I held the basket of smelly work clothes tight against my chest, fought back tears, and even managed to flash him a grin.

As I walked across the street, I held my head up high and tried to find a trace of dignity. I wanted people to think I'd offered to do my man's laundry, with my soap, the soap that I'd bought with my unemployment check. I was the only one fooled because as soon as I stepped into the house, my roommate let me have it.

"Puh-leeeeze, tell me those are not his clothes."

I pretended not to hear her and continued up the stairs, hoping that she would leave me alone. What was I thinking? That bitch tailed me and yelled at me like I was her child. She walked up the stairs behind me, keeping step with me, and told me to make his "very capable ass do his own damn laundry." When we got to the top of the stairs, she noticed that I didn't have soap in the basket.

"Please tell me that he gave you some laundry detergent. I didn't even do my boyfriend's laundry when he lived here. He didn't dare ask me, and you know why? Because that would've been total disrespect."

❖

She ranted for the next five minutes, scolding me as though I were a child. She gave me the most perfect "are you crazy look" between breaths. I tuned her out for the most part, only catching a few phrases, like "silly ass" and "crazy as hell."

After she finished adding to my misery, I laid across my bed, numb for the next few hours, without thought or movement, until I felt my daughter's hand tap me gently on my cheek. Kaiya leaned over and whispered in my ear, "Mommy, I'm hungry."

That evening I called the number on the card and it was the beautiful one who answered. I recognized his voice right away. When I asked for Carl, he said that Carl didn't live there. I was excited and confused. I identified myself and said, "Carl told me to call if my car continued to give me trouble."

"Carl was just trying to hook up with you," he said. "He lives at home with his wife and child."

There was an awkward pause.

"Does that mean he can't help me?" I didn't care about his living situation; I just needed help with my car.

He asked me my name again and then offered to help me himself. You can do more than help me, I thought.

I told him that after they'd left, my car stopped again, that I was unemployed, and that his brother had taken my last twenty bucks. I tried to sound as pitiful as I could because I needed my change back. He apologized repeatedly for Thomas's behavior.

"My brother, he's a hustler, but he's got a kind heart. If he'd known about your situation, he wouldn't have taken your money."

We made plans to meet at my car the next day. Would the rest of my money be there, too? I felt a lot

❖

better just knowing I was going to see the beautiful one.

The next morning, I woke up extra early to make sure I looked good. I wore a cute, tight red T, no bra (but on purpose that time) and a pair of tight denim shorts. I looked good leaving the house, but I had to walk to my car and it was hard to stay fresh in the heat and humidity.

I waited at the car for twenty minutes, and used the time to work on my pose. I settled for a humble seductress look. When he arrived, I flashed him a big smile to let him know how happy and appreciative I was for his assistance.

The first thing I noticed was his larger-than-life smile. His tall frame and confident walk commanded my attention. With a melodic, boyish laugh, he apologized for making me wait and said that he'd always had a problem with being punctual. I laughed too and assured him that it was okay.

His name was Noel and he went straight to work without much small talk. He connected jumper cables so he could give the car another boost. While waiting for the battery to charge, we snuck glances at each other. Finally, he broke the silence and asked me again about my tattoo. His gaze held mine as he waited for my response.

"I'd just lost a close friend from college that used to call me Angel," I said. "His wife shot him. She claimed post partum depression made her do it. He was a good guy and I miss him a lot."

"I'm sorry," Noel said.

"Some of my closest friends still call me Angel. I got it while visiting Miami with my family. I'd always wanted a tattoo and it was the smallest one in the shop. I wanted to make sure that I could take the pain.

❖

When they told me it meant Angel, I thought it was perfect."

"The name is perfect," he said, "for you."

He knew how to flash that beautiful smile. I was flattered when he told me that Angel suited me. I hoped that he was flirting with me but I wasn't sure.

His chin went on forever. He had beautiful, smooth skin, a moustache and full dark beard. His hair was in cornrows going back. He reminded me of the late, great Marvin Gaye.

Noel understood I had no money and made me feel as though he cared about what happened to me. It touched me that it was Saturday and he could've been anywhere, but chose to be there with me. Felix didn't offer to help but once Noel did, I didn't care.

I thanked him and told him that I didn't really have anyone else. I was going straight for sympathy because I hadn't seen any sign of my change and wanted to remind him how bad off I was.

"You got a man?" he asked.

His friend had asked that the day before and I'd evaded the question. But I was never one for lying, so I told the truth.

"He doesn't do much for me. We aren't getting along all that well. I barely see him."

I regretted my words the instant they passed my lips. Would Noel be like everyone else and put me down for staying with Felix?

He didn't. He just said that I deserved better. I nodded. I'd heard that before, but he surprised me by what he said next.

"I understand what you're going through. I've been there myself."

No one had said that to me before, even though most of the people I knew had put up with a miserable

❖

relationship at some point. It was also really striking to hear a guy admit that he'd done it, especially a man I'd just met.

The conversation paused while he disconnected the cables from each battery terminal. I stood there wondering why I couldn't let go of Felix and wishing that I could. I wanted so badly to walk away with no hesitation, but the very thought overwhelmed me with fear. Frustrated, I gave myself a little shake and snapped myself out of it. I preferred to bask in all of Noel's glory.

I drove home and he followed me in his car. We arrived at the house quickly and I was glad because I couldn't wait to continue our conversation. I wasn't thinking of my disabled car or any of my other problems. Once we got to the house, I gave him a glass of water because he had sweat through his clothes.

After about six hours of conversation, with a few diagnostic tests in between, he agreed with his brother that I needed a new starter. We jumped into his truck and went to the auto supply store. I walked closely behind him, acting as if I were his girlfriend. We continued to talk and laugh. He bought the starter and a few other parts and I thanked him.

We spent the rest of the evening discussing relationships, religion, philosophies, my kids, and his desire to have children. I told him I wanted to open a community center to help underserved families. The center would focus on the arts and technology and address issues that divide communities.

I hadn't had a conversation like this since I left college. He impressed me, leading me to look at things from a different perspective. He had a naive intelligence and simple, clear insights into complicated issues. His words captivated me and so

❖

did his spirit. He was so genuine and so kind. He was interested in my opinions and thought I was smart.

Six more hours went quickly. All of a sudden, he realized the time and began packing up his truck. It was going on midnight. The reality of my situation hit me and sadness overwhelmed me. Even after such a long day, I didn't want my day with him to end.

He asked if I were going to my cousin's house to pick up Kaiya. She usually let us stay over on the weekends because she knew how my roommate was and she felt sorry for us. But it was too late to fetch the kids. I decided to get them in the morning.

Noel was filthy after messing around with my car, but said he didn't feel comfortable about going into the house to wash up after I told him about the time Brandon came over to help me with the antenna on my TV. As soon as Brandon left, my roommate got out her oil and hit every corner of that apartment. She told me she couldn't stand strange men in her apartment and began speaking in tongues, making sure to put oil in each corner of the house to keep the evil man spirits out. I'd never seen anything like that before -- well, not for that reason anyway. Needless to say, there was no company for me after that.

Noel told me that he really enjoyed our conversation and that he felt like we'd known each other for years. I felt the same way. He asked if I wanted to continue to hang out.

I wasn't ready to leave him but I was praying he didn't want to go to a club. Orlando has a tight knit Caribbean community. I was nervous about Felix or one of his friends seeing me out. But I think I was more nervous about seeing Felix out with one of his new friends.

❖

Noel said that one of his friends was having a party and asked if I wanted to hang. A house party would be even worse when it came to the risk of being seen, but I agreed to go, anyway.

Track 8

Make Me A Woman

Make me a woman,
Whisper in my ear,
Take hold of my body,
Your touch like cashmere.

Make me a woman,
Hold me tight,
Caress me gently,
Kiss me right.

Make me a woman,
Take off my clothes,
Pull back the sheets,
Prepare to explode.
Make me a woman,
Stroke my face,

Adjust my hips,
Prepared for your embrace.

Make me a woman,
As you hold me close,
Mold me with your body,
Relaxed by your grace.

A woman.

I was willing to take the chance of being spotted out with Noel. I had a Love Jones strong. Noel left and I went to work, washing my goodies, oiling myself down and putting a dab of smell good in all the right places. I was excited about the possibilities but nervous about being out with another man. I was also nervous about the possibility of finding Felix out with another woman. He had been avoiding me like the plague.

I got to Noel's house in record time because I don't like to keep people waiting. I sat in the dark driveway for a couple of minutes to compose myself and took two long deep breaths to calm my nerves. I certainly didn't want to seem too eager; I needed to play it cool.

When ready, I knocked on the door and waited. Nothing happened. I knocked and waited some more, but there was no answer. All sorts of things went through my mind. Had he fallen asleep? Should I wake him? Or had he changed his mind? Was he watching from a window, waiting for me to leave, so he could go out without me? Then I remembered the great time we'd had and realized I was being silly.

Just as I was about to knock again, he opened the door, wearing nothing but a towel. How unfair was

❖

that? I fought every muscle in my face to keep from showing any reaction. That was a classic move. He was good. He had a tall, thin frame with defined muscles. I tried hard not to get caught checking him out so I did exactly what they taught me to do in graduate school after you've pictured your audience naked. I looked him straight in the eye and pretended not to be fazed by him at all.

He stood aside to let me in and complimented me on my perfume as I stepped past him. It was good that he liked it because Egyptian Musk was all I had at the time. His compliment was all it took for me to lose my composure. I smiled from ear to ear. He apologized for running late and of course I assured him that it was okay.

A dark hallway led to his bedroom. He said this was his brother's house and we should be quiet because Thomas was sleeping in the next room.

I sat on Noel's bed, expecting him to excuse himself to go and get dressed, but he sat down next to me.

"Do you really want to go to the party?" he asked. We could stay at his place and hang out instead, he said. He was tired, so I agreed to stay and hang out. He had worked hard all day. I, on the other hand, wasn't tired at all and was looking forward to more engaging conversation. But instead of conversation he asked for a massage. He was smiling from ear to ear.

Oh, my goodness! I had to perform already. We'd just met. I was nervous. He left the room to put his boxers on and brought back two beers. That cold beer was just what I needed. I chugged it down before he could even get comfortable.

❖

Looking concerned, he asked if I wanted another one. If I were going to give him a massage, I needed two or three more. I was nervous because I knew that intimate actions tend to lead to actions that are even more intimate.

We sat and talked for as long as it took me to drink the second beer. As soon as I put the empty bottle down he laid across his bed. It couldn't have been more obvious: he was ready for his massage. I straddled him to get into a better position and began to give him a deep tissue massage. I started at his neck and worked my way down.

This gave me the chance to finally check him out. His shoulders were broad and the muscles in his arms bulged as he crossed them under his face. The muscles in his face tensed and then relaxed every time I pressed into his skin. I could hear that he was enjoying the massage, too. Either his accent was getting stronger or I was getting tipsier because his voice sounded even nicer than before. He moaned and groaned every time I pressed into his flesh. By the time I reached the middle of his back, he was very relaxed. He allowed himself to get lost in the moment. He wasn't concerned about his brother in the next room anymore. He complimented me on how good my hands felt and then he reached around and started touching me.

"Awe, snooks," I said to myself.

His hands were squeezing my legs. By the time I got to the lower part of his back, I was into it as well. Somewhere between a moan and a groan, the massage became foreplay. I turned around to massage the lower part of his body. He began touching my tummy, so I elongated my spine and flexed my abs so he couldn't feel the rolls caused by me slumping over. He

❖

moved up to my breast and I massaged around his mid-thigh, attempting to arouse him further. He let out a deep moan and I realized then that it was on. I went deeper between his legs and found exactly what I was looking for. There it was, in all its glory, except it was much more glorious than I had expected.

"What is that?" I asked.

He asked me what I was talking about, so I squeezed harder to show him exactly what the concern was about.

He laughed. There was nothing boyish about his laugh that time. I had awakened the man. After another ten minutes of exploration, we became absorbed in each other's touch and escaped to another place.

It didn't take long for my moans to become groans, and more intense with every touch. He placed me on the bed next to him. He gazed at me with that intense stare of his, contemplating his next move.

It's all right, I thought, gazing back at him, hoping to connect telepathically.

It was a powerful moment. No words can explain the way I felt. He gripped the small of my back and pulled me closer to him. He kissed my lips, my neck, and my face. I couldn't believe what was happening. I grabbed him tightly, my tummy filled with butterflies as my entire body tightened in anticipation of the most beautiful and intense release I had ever experienced. It was like an out-of-body experience. We were still in the middle of foreplay and I couldn't believe that his touch could be so arousing. I had never experienced anything like it. I was hooked, like a drug addict having her first high.

We made love all night long. I woke up early the next morning, but Noel slept on, until about mid-

❖

afternoon. He was exhausted from the night's activities, but I felt energized.

I went to my cousin Penny's house and told her all about Noel. I took her through a minute-by-minute account of the day. I told her how we'd spent the evening together and that he was so beautiful and sweet. I must have gazed off, lost in thought, because I heard her shout, "What did you do?"

She was just as excited as I was. I referred to Noel as my guardian angel. She entertained me for as long as I needed. My cousin and I were like little schoolgirls. She enjoyed living vicariously through my stories.

Noel and I spent every day of the next two weeks together. I let my guard down. I felt free. He would sneak over pizza with pineapples while my roommate was at work. When the kids were outside or watching a movie, he and I would tip toe away for some alone time.

We had the most fun talking and napping under the weeping willow trees at my favorite park. We reminisced about our first time together. We dozed on and off as a cool breeze caressed our faces. We watched cricket tournaments and he explained the game to me. He invited the kids and me over to watch movies to give us some relief from my crazy roommate and he cooked real Jamaican food for us. He cooked red beans and rice, Callaloo, fried plantains and cabbage.

We took long drives at night and would end up in some deserted parking lot to talk and stare at the moon. He told me that he wanted lots of kids of his own and would give them names that started with the letter "N" so everyone would know they belonged to him.

❖

We were big dreamers with big hearts. He talked about educating the youth in his country and putting an end to the violence. I talked about ideas for my community center and calling it "The Angels' Village." He sparked an energy and drive in me I'd forgotten I had.

Everything was perfect.

Then, after two weeks of bliss, he told me his time was up.

"What does that mean?" I asked.

"My visa is expiring. I have to go back to Jamaica in three days."

I almost swallowed my tongue.

He said he'd never met anyone like me, and that he wasn't ready for our time to end, but had no choice. He could tell that I was stunned, so he put his arms around me for comfort.

"I'm not sure when I'm coming back," he said. "I'm planning to enroll in the university."

I tuned him out after that. I heard him talking but I don't know what he was saying. I didn't know whether to act like I didn't care, drop to his feet and beg him not to go, or slap him in his face for waiting until the last minute to tell me. He let me fall in love with him, knowing that he would be leaving. I did the only thing I knew how to do. I put my coat of armor back on and acted as if I didn't care.

I don't remember what happened the days before he left. However, I do remember our not-so-sweet good-bye.

We hugged and then I pulled back. I couldn't look at him. He asked me to come closer but I refused.

"Angel, I'll miss you so much."

He tried to hug me again but I pulled away. I was having a hard time handling the situation. I

❖

wanted to cry, but I was tired of crying. I still couldn't look him in the eyes, so I stared at the ground.

"Please, just let me hold you," he said.

So I did. I allowed him to hug me but I couldn't return it. I just tapped him on the back, and then moved away again. I meant to make that good-bye as quick and painless as possible.

Was I being punished for seeing Noel behind Felix's back? But how could that be? I'd only talked to Felix twice since meeting Noel and one of those times was when he came to pick up his laundry.

Noel tried to kiss me but I stepped back again. I was angry with him and angry with myself. I just wanted him to leave.

He gave me a card with his home and email address. I put it in my back pocket, certain that I'd never speak to him or see him again. I had no phone to make long distance calls, couldn't afford a stamp, and sure as hell couldn't afford a computer.

Noel wanted to have a long, heartfelt good-bye, but my bruised heart wouldn't let me. I stepped back from him to make sure he understood. We stood next to his truck for another ten minutes, making small talk, before he finally had to leave.

I took a deep breath and forced myself to look at him without emotion. Then I wished him well and told him to have a safe trip. He made one last and final attempt to kiss me, but I wouldn't let him. He got in the truck and drove away. I stood there until he was out of sight.

❖

Track 9

On the Edge

I sit here in silence,
Playing a game of Russian roulette,
Both hands grip tight.
One bullet called love,
Finger on the trigger,
Daydreaming,
Contemplating,
Laughing,
Crying,
Wrestling life,
Staggering on the edge,
Falling out of balance,
I'm out of control.
My love for you is strong,
It penetrates my soul.

My weak mind,
My weak heart,
My weak faith,
Is gonna keep me playing the fool.
I'm stronger than this,
I can pull myself through,
"Live better, pray harder, love lighter,"
A daily mantra of mine.

Not a day went by when I didn't think about Noel. I pictured his long skinny fingers and the pronounced brow that made him look serious even when he was laughing. My memories offered relief and helped me get through the lonely times. They weren't enough though, so I began writing poetry to express my feelings. I was finally able to let out years of private pain. Every bit of the pain and sorrow and love poured out. My poems reflected my state of mind. Writing saved my life; he saved my life. I was and will forever be grateful to him for that.

I'd always been a hopeless romantic. I really believed I would find my king and live happily ever after. At the time, I believed a force guided the path I took the morning I met Noel, one that was too powerful for me to understand. Our paths crossed for very specific reasons. I'd met the man who would teach me wonderful life lessons about what it felt like to be appreciated. In so doing, he would change my life forever. He was a gift from God. I didn't become jaded until a few years later.

Two days after Noel left, my roommate told me she didn't trust me in her house while she was at work. I was shocked.

"Do you really think I'd steal from you?" I asked.

❖

She said she hadn't realized how difficult it would be to share her space. She never asked me to leave, but it was obvious that it was time for me to go.

An hour later, my cousin Penny and her kids came over to bring us lunch. I put up a front, pretending that nothing was wrong, but my insides were in knots. I felt sick to my stomach. I didn't know what to do. After about ten minutes, the pressure was too much and I broke down. While the kids were eating at the table I dropped to my knees, covered my face, and wept. I cried hard, but silently so as not to upset them. My eyes and throat hurt from the pressure as I fought from making any sound.

Penny didn't know what to do. She watched me melt deeper and deeper into the floor before asking me what was wrong. I told her what had happened and she repeated her invitation for us to come and live with her family. I had been telling her no for months, but this time I had no choice. I agreed.

I moved into her apartment at the end of October. I knew it was a mistake. She had a crazy husband and two kids and her place had just enough space for them. I was in the way again. My children and I had to all sleep on the living room couch. There wasn't even a door we could shut for some privacy.

Even though living in her apartment was so cramped, it did make me feel a lot better. She and I laughed a lot together. It was like reliving our childhood. My bones didn't hurt as much. She helped me find humor in my situation. Now I would laugh to keep from crying. I applied for work anywhere and everywhere. I sold perfume door-to-door and sought work at a gas station – we laughed about that. I finally landed a part-time position at a pet store. The job paid minimum wage and we laughed some more.

❖

A month after the kids and I moved in, Penny's husband moved out and bought a half-million dollar house with his girlfriend. Penny couldn't wait to tell me that her dad blamed me for her problems with her husband. I reminded her that after she left her husband two years earlier, I let her and her rotten-to-the-core children live in my tiny two-bedroom apartment. And when her husband left the military to be with them, he moved in as well.

"Penny, us moving in here may have been his last straw, but by no means are we the reason he left."

We haven't laughed together since.

I would've never made her feel bad about stressing me the hell out. I certainly wouldn't have told her if Mom had a negative thought about her staying there. That's family for you. My only option was to go to a shelter, but I wasn't that proud, so I stayed right there in her apartment.

I couldn't stand my job at the pet store. My manager, Becky, looked at me as if I were scum. She wouldn't even speak to me. I knew she was young because she wore her jeans skintight with fifty cheap plastic bracelets on her arms. Her hair was in a just-rolled-out-of-bed ponytail. I was there an entire month before she found out I was in my late twenties with a master's degree. Then she gave me the same "Are you crazy?" look my roommate gave me for doing a grown man's dirty laundry.

During my lunch break, she asked me what I was doing there.

"I need to feed my kids," I said.

She and my co-worker clucked and commented about what they'd do if they had my education. I was embarrassed and ashamed. I wanted to remind them that I was still in the room.

❖

But I just kept quiet.

These people had no idea how much pain and rage I felt. For all they knew, I could've been a recovering crack addict. As I sat there in the lunchroom, half-listening to them, I was very sure of one thing: it was only by the grace of God that I didn't slap the both of them bald.

Meanwhile, Felix was becoming even more distant. He offered little comfort or relief. I didn't want much. A little conversation to take me away from my issues for a while would have been nice, but he always made me feel worse. He never allowed me to cry or become overwhelmed in front of him. It made him feel uncomfortable. He didn't think I had reason to cry because what I was enduring was something that many people endure at one time or another.

Felix didn't realize that I was also mourning the loss of the love of my life and was sad to be stuck there with him. Every time it looked like I was going to cry, Felix would get extremely uncomfortable. His entire body would tense. His forehead would get a deep crease between his eyes, making him look angry. Sometimes, I felt sorrier for him than I did for myself, but then he would break out with another one of his sorry speeches. They were getting worse and sounded like half-time locker room cheers. He would tell me, "Don't cry about it," "be strong" and "hold your head up," then end it with, "Show them what you're made of."

After my half-time cheer, I'd just stare at him. I tried to work up enough courage to ask him for five dollars for gas or a loaf of bread and some peanut butter, but I never did. I hated feeling like a burden and wanted him to offer his help, but he never did.

❖

It took me another three months to get back on my feet. In January 2001, I started working for "The Neighborhood Village," an organization that provided kids with an alternative to running the streets. I was back in Pine Hills serving the community that I loved. I was excited to be a part of it because it was my life's passion to give back, and not just to kids, but families as well. The position didn't pay much, but I was able to save enough money to move into a small one-bedroom apartment.

Noel and I had talked about doing this kind of work and I wanted to tell him about it. So I got my phone turned on and called Jamaica as soon as I heard a dial tone. I couldn't catch up with him though. I called every week or so for about a month. His father told me that he was at work in another part of Jamaica and didn't come home often.

Meanwhile, I threw myself into my work. It was a startup program and it was my responsibility to recruit families to open their home to the kids in their community. Each family would get a computer, snacks, and training. It sounded like a great idea. I walked through neighborhoods in hot, humid 90-degree heat to beg generous souls to open their doors – and ran into the same challenges most inner cities face. Some people didn't trust the program, or me, or couldn't pass the background check, usually because of a child abuse or drug charge. Some worked two jobs and weren't home enough to care for their own children, let alone someone else's.

It was slow going even after I found great volunteers. I would host grand openings to advertise a new Neighborhood Village house opening and couldn't even get the kids next door to show up. Change does take time but I didn't understand how

❖

anyone could let free food go to waste. The volunteers and I would sit outside all day, watching the hotdogs get cold and the soda get hot. But after a few months, word got around and then we had to turn kids away.

By that time, Felix and I were pretty much over. He knew I was moving into my new apartment, but of course he didn't offer to help. I didn't expect him to. I hadn't seen him for a week and a half and we rarely spoke on the phone anymore. There was a time when he wouldn't go a day without seeing me, or a few hours without calling.

My depression was still there; I couldn't shake it. It was still very difficult for me to support my kids properly. Having no support system was taking its toll. I have always been stubbornly independent and couldn't stand asking for help even when I desperately needed it. My emotional state had taken a toll on me physically. Once my insurance kicked in, I went to see a doctor and was prescribed a drug to help stabilize my mood. I never took it. I couldn't get past needing prescription drugs to help me with my mood. Looking back on it, I realize how foolish it was to think that. After all, I had no problem depending on alcohol to get me through rough patches.

To take up my time after work and before bed, I got a gym membership and invested in yoga DVDs for home. I worked out two hours a day, six days a week in the gym, and would do Yoga every time I found myself wallowing in self-pity. The effects of months of inactivity and stress were obvious. I was twenty-five pounds overweight. My eyes were lifeless, with dark circles and bags underneath. My skin was dull and my hair dry and brittle. I needed something to get me out of this rut. I needed to be out among the living.

❖

It was February. Orlando would host Carnival in three months and I wanted to be ready. I ran three miles every other day and lifted weights on the days in-between. I lost the twenty-five pounds plus seven more.

Carnival was held during the last weekend in May. It coincided with the last day of school. Everyone was ready for relief from the hustle and bustle of everyday life. Fetes were being held all over town and I attended a few. I loved to dance and I could wine it up with the best of them.

I saw a few mutual friends of Felix's and mine. They knew what was going on between us because Felix loved to tell our business, especially if it had anything to do with closed-door activities. Little did any of them know that our sex life was mediocre at best. His body had fallen apart. Years earlier, he'd been in a car accident. As a result, his left knee wouldn't let him move very well, and he suffered from headaches daily because of his high blood pressure. Most of the time, sex with Felix was kind of funny. He would behave like an 80-year-old attached to an oxygen tank while I worked up all kinds of sweat. He would lie there with his face twisted in all directions and when it got really good for him, his eyes would roll back and he would mumble, "It's so sweet." If he were getting ready to prematurely release – usually after about seventeen minutes – he would grab my waist and say, "Wait! Wait! Wait!"

I would stop moving for about thirty-five seconds, allowing his pressure to go down, and then he would give me permission to continue. After that, it wouldn't take more than ten more minutes to finish him off.

Ahh, those were the old good days.

I wouldn't have ever humiliated him the way he did me. I had retained more of our friend's. Men and women would tell me what I was doing in the bedroom. I wanted to tell them that it wasn't as eventful as he made it sound.

A few of Felix's friends propositioned me because he ran his mouth. One of them had the nerve to call my house and invite me out. Another friend, Clyde, would tell me everything Felix was doing. Apparently, Felix had been dating another woman. Well, at least, he was telling her business now and not mine. He loved country and western music and had finally found someone to take to Cowboys, the most popular country and western club in Orlando. He'd taken me a few times but, with my dark skin and dread locks, I stood out badly. The stares and the pressure to line dance made me feel extremely uncomfortable. He was too clueless and infatuated with honkekkdfasod honkey-tonk music, tight, high-waisted Wrangler jeans, big belt buckles and cowboy boots to notice.

I did allow Clyde to take me out – once. We didn't go too far but I guess we did cross the line. I wanted to pay Felix back for three years of treating me like crap and then throwing me away when I was down. Felix once told me he'd had a nightmare in which his boss and I were seeing each other. I didn't think that was the best time to tell him to start trusting his instincts.

During one of the Carnival fetes, I pretended nothing was wrong. I had a few beers and mingled in the crowed. I tried to spot Felix but it was so crowded that he would've had no problem hiding from me. I knew he was there; he never missed a good fete.

❖

I danced and drank all night. The later it got, the drunker I was, and pretty soon it felt like no one was on the dance floor but my partner and I. His name was David. He was American-born, but Trini to the bone and you couldn't tell him otherwise. He was an accountant from Boston and was only in town for the weekend. We had a great connection. His body moved perfectly in sync with mine. We had an audience and I knew my good time would get back to Felix if he weren't already watching me. I didn't care.

The night ended at about 4 a.m. David and I were standing by my car talking, when Clyde came over and asked if I was okay. I said I was fine and he left, but I wasn't okay and I knew it. I was drunk.

The next thing I remember was waking up in my living room floor at about 11:00 a.m. I had no idea how I'd gotten there. I spent the rest of the day suffering from a mean hangover and swore I'd never drink like that again.

I got the kids up early Sunday to see the Carnival parade. Of course, it started four hours late. We stood along the side of the road under the hot sun and watched the performers mash it up for another two hours. Then I took the kids back home and waited for the sun to set before going back out to enjoy the evening festivities. Every year I looked forward to seeing the band Mystic NRB and the lead singer Craig Camacho perform the "Dollar Wine" song. Camacho would invite people from the crowd to show off their big money wine. I always wanted to go up but didn't because it doesn't look as good on small hips and I didn't want to embarrass myself.

When I got there I saw Felix sitting on a blanket in the middle of the festival field with Rufus and Trudy, his godparents. Felix pretended not to notice me. That pissed me off and I wanted to piss him off. So I chugged rum straight from a friend's flask, trying to get a quick buzz. I was too impatient and drank way too much. I flirted with everyone. Felix still paid me no mind. Hours went by and I continued to play my pathetic games between more shots of rum. The next thing I remember was a rocking motion. I opened my eyes to find Felix carrying me. I was only conscious for a few seconds.

I woke up the next morning, confused. I didn't know how I'd gotten to Felix's house. I asked Felix what had happened. He told me that Clyde saw me passed out and that he took me to the First Aide tent. I lay there for a while and tried to remember, but I couldn't. I did remember talking to Clyde in the parking lot, though.

Then Felix started kissing me. I was still groggy from the night before and couldn't respond. I have never been able to stand kisses first thing in the morning. Keep a glass of mouthwash by the bed and rinse first for goodness' sakes.

I held my breath for about three minutes. Then he climbed on top of me. I was still too dazed to respond. He made several attempts to get me to position myself for him but I just lay there. He finally got frustrated enough to give up. He looked disgusted with me. I couldn't stand his look of disapproval. I've always tried to make everyone happy, no matter how it cost me. That's been my biggest problem. So, before he could get up, I grabbed his arm, pulled him close, and wrapped my legs around him.

Afterward, we got up to have breakfast and talked about what was going on between us.

"Why are you ignoring me?" I asked.

"I'm not."

❖

"What about all those times I called? You never called back."

"I've been working a lot of extra hours and I'm tired, tired all the time."

Felix always used work as an excuse. I didn't press him but I was getting more and more upset. He didn't even respect me enough to tell the truth. He didn't know his friends had already told me what he was doing.

We continued the conversation on the way to my apartment. The drive home was tense. I finally let him know that I'd heard some of the things he was doing. He denied all of it. Once we got to my apartment, I got out of the car and got downright belligerent. I got loud so he reached over and tried to pinch me on my side to get me to lower my voice, like I was a three-year-old. I pushed his hand away, so he tried grabbing me to calm me down. I ran in circles because I knew he couldn't catch me. He tried to chase me, and thought the whole thing was funny—— until he blew his knee out.

"You're acting like a child," he said, bent over his hood, huffing and puffing and grimacing in pain.

I felt sorry for him but thought he deserved every bit of it. Neither one of us said anything else. I walked into the house to nurse another hangover. I asked God what had happened to me, begged for His help, took two Tylenol and slept the rest of the day.

I beat myself up for weeks after that. I was incredibly embarrassed and upset that I'd given Felix something else to talk about. How could I have let it happen? At night, I would force myself to sleep to avoid facing what I'd done: I had lost control. When sleep didn't come, I'd reflect. Why did people who

❖

were supposed to love me find it so easy to discard me? Why didn't they fight to keep me around?

When I was about six years old, Leroy, the man I thought was my father came to visit from Cleveland. I was so excited. When he got out of the car, Naja and I burst through the front door and ran to him, screaming "Daddy! Daddy!"

Naja got to him first. He scooped her up and gave her a big hug.

Running down the walkway, arms extended, I was ready to jump and have him take me into his arms, too. Instead, when I got to him, he dodged me, as if I were a ball that had been thrown at him. I ran right passed him and my knees buckled as I tried to stop myself from falling. I couldn't understand what had happened. I turned around, confused, and saw him walk inside the house without even looking back to make sure I was okay.

When Leroy left, I asked Mom why he didn't act like I was his daughter. She told me because they were divorced before I was born. That was the only discussion we had about him.

My father didn't fight to put his name on my birth certificate or for me to know who he was. He lived a few blocks from us and was at our house every weekend sipping on Crown Royal. I had no idea who he was to me other than a family friend until I was about eleven and my cousin, Veeshous, from out of town came to visit.

There we were, on the front steps hanging out, talking about a whole lot of nothing, when out of nowhere came, "You know Rob's your daddy?"

I'll never forget that moment.

Before I moved to Orlando, I went to visit my so-called daddy. I felt a need to connect with him after

❖

my ordeal with Antonio. I was searching for my foundation and my self-worth. I needed to know I was important to him.

The weekend was going great. For the first time in twenty-seven years I felt like I understood where my sense of humor and carefree spirit came from. He made me laugh a lot. I was privileged to see his sacred "man room". It was full of guns, the floor carpeted with girly magazines. He made me promise not to tell anyone that he shot squirrels from the window. I pictured him in full-face paint and fatigues having flashbacks of the war singing maritime songs.

I pitied his wife Maudine. She was a God fearing woman and Rob didn't celebrate holidays or birthdays for that matter. Mother's Day brunch was spent with girlfriends and Christmas at her daughter's. The weekend was fun and effortless until I asked one too many questions about his other children. He looked at me with frustration.

"Why do you want to know?" he asked. "What difference does it make?"

The atmosphere became tense. He saw my surprise and that I had been embarrassed into silence.

That moment was one of several that shaped me. I wasted many years after that, searching for a new mold. Thinking back, I remember how I tried to keep a safe distance from my college friend Lei and her parents. I pushed them away, while I desperately tried to make my own family work, to fix relationships not worth fixing. In spite of my lack of responsiveness, Lei, Alfonza and Savannah called and sent cards for my birthday every year, and never missed a holiday. They would look high and low for me when I would loose touch. They never gave up on me.

❖

I didn't expect my father to announce me to the rest of the family or hope for an emotional reunion. I just wanted to get to know him. But I tried to force twenty-seven years into a single weekend and it overwhelmed him.

I understood that he grew up at a time when having children out of wedlock was taboo and I understood the need to keep it a secret out of shame. But being the child of such a union, I also understood how it felt to be fatherless. I haven't seen or spoken to him since. I measured my self-worth by his rejection and it took a long time before I stopped doing that.

For years I felt sad for my daughter because her father wasn't doing all he could to have a relationship with her. I tried my best to foster a relationship between them and made sure that she never heard a bad word spoken against him because I didn't want her to grow up feeling thrown away the way I did.

But once she reached a certain age, I also realized that I couldn't do all of the work for him. I had to let him do it himself, not for his sake, but for her's.

❖

Interlude

You

You inspire me,
Intrigue me,
And delight me.

You

Track 10

Your Man Took Me

He lied,
He cheated,
Played us both for fools.
Why can't you see
That I'm a victim too?
But you still tell yourself
I was the cause.
Listen when I say
It wasn't me at all.
Why can't you see?
I couldn't take your man,
Because while you were away
He was too busy taking me.
He spoke of love.

He told all his friends
I was sent from above.
You were apart
For so many years,
And now you want to start
Questioning what he's doing here.
You turned a blind eye,
And a deaf ear,
And hoped it was a lie.
All of our friends
Think I did you wrong,
But the only thing I'm guilty of
Is being in love.
He was committed to you,
But I didn't have a clue.
I said it once; I'll say it again:
I couldn't have taken your man,
'Cause he was too busy taking me.

The kids went to Virginia to visit their grandma for the rest of the summer, so life would be a little easier for the next couple of months. I spent my time writing, mostly at night when it was quiet and I couldn't run from my thoughts. I was lost and ashamed and incredibly lonely. I spent countless nights lying in bed weeping. I tried to keep quiet so my neighbors wouldn't hear me. My eyes were bloodshot, my face tightened and veins protruded from my forehead and neck and my throat burned holding back the pain. I felt like a junkie going through detox.

I hadn't heard from Felix. I called once and left a message but he didn't return it and I was okay with it. I didn't intend to call again. I didn't care anymore and was exhausted. The heaviness was overpowering.

❖

Three weeks after Felix and I fought in the street, he showed up at my job unannounced. I was shocked. Did he want closure? Did he want me back? Did he want to check up on me to make sure I was okay?

He greeted me and asked if we could go somewhere to talk. We walked outside and I braced myself for what he was going to say. He told me he'd gotten a call from Dorthea.

Dorthea was his wife. I knew he was married but I thought it was the same situation as mine, so I never questioned him. For almost three years, I'd visited him at his house whenever I wanted to. He had no pictures of her or his kids around and she never called. What would her call have to do with me?

"She called from Tobago," he said. "She'll be flying into Miami in the morning."

Then I understood. He was afraid I'd call and jack his ass up. Dorthea and the kids came up every summer from Tobago and it had never been an issue before. This time, he hadn't had time to prepare me.

"Please, don't call the house," he said.

When we first met, I'd asked him if I could take his daughters to get their nails done or shopping at the mall. He said his kids wouldn't be able to handle seeing him with another woman, so I never met them. I respected that. Even though Felix and I were dating, my daughter never knew it. I was very careful of what she saw and I thought he was doing the same. I guess I should've asked at least one question.

After I got home the next day, I found an unfamiliar female voice on my answering machine. There were two messages and both sounded serious.

She introduced herself as Dorthea, Felix's wife. She told me that she wanted to talk to me "woman to

❖

woman." She assured me that she didn't want to fight, just talk, and asked me to please call her back. She had a soft voice with a deep accent. I didn't think twice about it, just picked up the phone and called her back.

"Ayo?" she asked as soon as she picked up. Once I confirmed my identity she asked me to come and get her right away before Felix got home. Before I could hang up, she asked me if I knew how to delete calls from the caller ID. She was afraid Felix would learn that she'd called me.

Felix had a high tech phone that I could barely work myself. It had taken me two months to figure out how to use the most basic functions. So I had no idea how to help her.

I couldn't believe I was going to meet her. I changed clothes quickly, picking out an outfit that was as flattering as possible. I needed to look my best when she sized me up.

I got to the house later than expected and was very nervous. I just knew Felix would pull up behind me. Dorthea was waiting by the window and came out as soon as she saw me pull to a stop in front of the house.

She was pretty. Her short haircut was tapered in the back and she had dark chocolate skin, like mine. She was much heavier on the bottom than I was though. I had run every ounce of curve from my hips in the gym. (I was regretting that because I didn't have much to begin with.) She was older than I was. It was clear just from the way she wore her clothes. She wore Capri's with her belt fastened high above her navel with her buttoned-down sleeveless shirt tucked in. I remembered thinking that you can't even find high-wasted pants anymore.

❖

I thought meeting her would be awkward but it wasn't. As soon as she got in the car, she suggested that we go somewhere to talk before Felix got home. She was nervous. I was nervous, too, but I kind of wanted to see Felix's face.

"I recognized you right away," she said. "Felix has a picture of you in a drawer with your tattoo showing."

It surprised me that he still had my picture on display. I kept quiet but drove as slowly as I could, without being obvious, hoping that he would pass us on the street.

She looked harmless, but I prepared for the worse because I know that hell hath no furry like a woman scorned. I remembered driving by his house with my headlights off fantasizing about putting bologna on Felix's car, so it would eat the paint off, and dropping Snicker bars into his gas tank. The only reason I didn't do either was because I was afraid of getting caught.

So I was waiting on her to start beating the crap out of me while I drove down Colonial Drive. I decided to go to the mall where there would be witnesses if she decided she wanted to fight.

I took her to the Florida Mall. We sat in the food court, constantly looking over our shoulders. My adrenalin was pumping, heart bouncing against my chest and palms dripping with sweat.

"How long have you been dating my husband?" she asked.

I told her the truth, but I didn't say that for the last year we were only together for his pleasure. I couldn't believe what came out of her mouth after that.

❖

She said that Felix had been involved with many women. She'd met twelve of them, including me. My stomach was in knots and she was visibly shaken. I felt sorry for her.

Felix had come to the States, she said, to make a better life for her and the kids, but he'd stopped calling and hadn't respond to her emails for some time. So she'd come to find out what he was up to.

She gave me that same pitiful look I had when I was trying to get my money back from Thomas. I sympathized with her but wondered why she spent so much money to find out what her husband was doing. She already knew, and apparently didn't mind eleven women ago. Her 13-year-old daughter had told her to leave him for good if she found out that he was having another affair. Something told me that would never happen.

She described how she'd fought with a woman he had been seeing. She must've lost that fight because she'd taken a very different tactic with me. She said she'd left him once and moved to Canada with the kids. He chased her there and she thought they had patched things up. Then he began having an affair with a Canadian girl.

She told me everything and I knew she was telling me the worst of the worst to turn me against him. The final blow for me was when she said that a man had broken into their home while she and the kids slept and Felix was spending the night with another woman. Then she added one last ugly truth to make sure I was totally disgusted: Apparently he had been laid up with another woman the night she gave birth to their youngest.

I could tell she was praying that I would do the right thing and leave her man alone. Her arms were

❖

folded across her chest and she was looking in my eyes for some sign of compassion. I assured her that she didn't have to worry about me because Felix and I hadn't been seeing each other for a while.

We bonded over the next thirty minutes, sharing our bad Felix stories. We made fun of the tarter in his teeth and his horrible sexual skills. On the way up from Miami they argued and he had the nerve to tell her that he wasn't sexually attracted to her.

She told me that I was too young to be dealing with any of his crap and that I should find a man to treat me right. Privately, I wondered, "Why don't you take your own advice and leave?"

When she remembered that I told her that I'd been dating her husband for the past three years, she lost it. It hit her that everyone in Felix's circle had known about the both of us and said nothing.

"Those lying bastards!" she cried.

Her sorrow turned into hatred. Her so-called friends had smiled in her face and told her he wasn't seeing anyone else every time she'd gone to visit.

"Liars! They're all liars!" she shouted.

She was starting to attract attention, but she didn't care. Her voice had gotten deeper and she was trembling.

We decided to visit everyone we knew who had been lying to us.

Felix's job was first on the list. I pulled into the driveway and parked directly behind Felix's car. Dorthea got out and stormed inside. Sixty seconds later, Felix rushed her back outside, using the rear entrance. Sitting inside the car, I heard him call me every nasty name in the book.

Then he told her that I was "just something to do."

❖

I was hurt, but not surprised. His was a normal reaction for someone who was caught cheating. Once he noticed that my car was parked behind his, he got into his and backed up, forcing me to do the same. Dorthea jumped into mine, and the chase was on. I couldn't keep up with him, though. I wasn't as brave behind the wheel as he was. He weaved in and out of rush hour traffic to get us off his tail.

Once he was out of sight, Dorthea asked me to pull over so she could use the pay phone. She called Felix's boss and mentor, Rufus. Rufus owned the electrical company Felix worked for and told Felix what to do about every aspect of his life.

I couldn't stand that man. Rufus bought the house that Felix was renting. Felix told me that Rufus was the reason I couldn't move in when I had no place to go. He made no decisions without consulting Godfather Rufus.

Rufus's wife, Trudy, answered the phone. Upset and excited, Dorthea spoke in a rush. Her accent got so thick I could barely understand her. What I did understand, however, is that she accused Trudy of having lied to her face.

Once Dorthea chewed Trudy out, we went to another mutual "friend's" house. You should've seen the black leave Wanda's face when she opened the door. She played it off well but Wanda never looked you in the eye. When she'd talked to you she looked up and to the left.

They hugged as if they were old friends reacquainting themselves. We brought Wanda up to speed. She admitted that she knew about the both of us. Wanda was enjoying this. She decided to call Lucinda.

❖

Now, Lucinda went by the nickname of "Bonnie," presumably because her husband's name was Clyde. I'd met Bonnie through Felix. She owned a dance studio and I'd enrolled my daughter there. Wanda had a daughter enrolled in the dance school as well.

"Bonnie, what cha doin?" Wanda said. "Come over here now. You won't believe this." Wanda giggled like a little schoolgirl.

Bonnie must have been near by, because she was there in less than ten minutes. She didn't look that surprised when she saw Dorthea. By then, word had spread.

"Felix called me," Bonnie said. "He was frantic. I couldn't calm him down. He was freaking out."

She burst out laughing. In fact, we were all in tears, laughing.

Wanda and Bonnie told stories about how they both knew about Dorthea and me, and how awkward it was for them and their families.

"I remember the last time you were here," Bonnie told Dorthea. "You and Felix came to the house with the kids. My daughter said, 'Mommy where are Felix's other children?' We all knew Ayo first," she said, gesturing to me. "We met Ayo a year before we met you."

Bonnie never invited me to her house.

I was glad Bonnie said that. It was important for Dorthea to realize that I was a victim, too.

We continued to talk and plot against Felix, hyping ourselves up. Bonnie was the ringleader. She wanted to get him where it hurt. Dorthea thought she should call immigration and make him come home. We laughed some more. The next thing I knew Bonnie had the phonebook on her lap and was looking up the

❖

number for immigration. They all designated me to call. I was nervous but the pressure was on. They kept saying they didn't think I would leave Felix. I had to prove that I was serious. Everyone was quiet while I made the call.

It was interesting to see them get excited at the idea of Felix being deported. Not two weeks ago, they were all partying with him at Carnival. Over the years, I'd learned that every single husband in our circle was adulterous. All the wives knew it too. Maybe, they were using that moment to express years of their own private pain.

Wanda was the only one, besides me, who expressed qualms about what we were doing. I agreed with her to a point, but I parted with her when she said that we were messing with a man's respect. I got angry. No one seemed to care about a woman's respect, I said. We didn't know it then, but eventually, Wanda's husband would leave her. Did she feel the same way, then?

I made the call. When I hung up, I told the others what I'd learned: Immigration said they couldn't do anything unless we could prove that Felix had committed a crime. That was pre 9/11.

I was relieved. I hadn't wanted to make that call. Bonnie asked me not to tell her husband that she was involved with calling immigration because he would be vexed. I hadn't intended to do so. I knew our bonding session was just for show.

It was getting late so I dropped Dorthea off at Felix's place and went home. I resumed my daily routine of running, writing poems and reflecting on why my life had become such a mess.

Two weeks later, Dorthea sent me an email. She was back in Tobago, hoped I was okay and had

❖

moved on with my life. We exchanged emails for about a month and even joked about writing a book together about our experience, but nothing ever came of it.

Track 11

Fed Up

I swear if I didn't wake up this morning,
No one would care.
If my heart just stopped beating,
There would be one less burden to bear.
I'm struggling for my survival,
For my piece of mind.
If one more person says something to me,
I'm gonna punch 'em in the eye.
I ain't ever felt like fighting
More than I do right now,
Except when I found the hair in my bed
My ex-husband's lover left behind.
I am so tired of being hurt.
I want to crawl in a hole and die,
Because I can't seem to find the reason why

God put on this earth.
The one person who loves me
Lives across the sea.
I wish he'd come and rescue me
From this crazy life I see,
Because I might do something I'll regret
And have to take the insanity plea.

By the end of June, a month after the Carnival and the Felix madness, I was finally able to buy a computer and couldn't wait to send Noel an email. I missed the spirit-filled conversations, the all-night talks about saving the world, and how we laughed about absolutely nothing together. Nothing had been the same for me since he'd left. Did he intend to come back to the States? I was ready to do whatever it took to get him back to me.

When he wrote me back, almost a month later, I was so nervous I needed about two weeks before I could respond. "Noel Wellington," it said in the subject line of my inbox. I couldn't believe it. An entire year had passed since he left. He was working five hours from his home in Kingston and only went home the last weekend of each month. The best part was that he gave me the phone number to the house he was renting. He warned, however, that it might be hard to get through. He shared the phone with other tenants and said I shouldn't call after 9:30 p.m.

He also mentioned that he was on a contract that could turn into permanent employment with a construction firm. That word "permanent" didn't make me happy. He was working on the North Coast Highway Development as the chief surveyor on site and didn't know when he'd back to Orlando.

❖

He said it was good to know that Felix and I had finally broken up and he reminded me that I deserved someone who would encourage me in all of my endeavors. He added that he was in a similar predicament. He and the girl he was dating didn't have the spiritual connection that he and I shared.

It was nice to have finally heard from him. I was in a better place after I'd read his email. So many negative thoughts and people had been consuming me. It was nice to get lost in his words.

The next few months were rough. I couldn't connect with Noel on a regular basis. The only calls I did receive were from Bonnie to make sure I was still calling immigration, but after a couple of weeks, they stopped too. Those women abandoned me after pretending to be my new BFFs. They put on a great show for Dorthea's sake, but they were hypocrites. Even though they couldn't stand Felix, they encouraged his behavior and protected him. They protected Dorthea. They were friends with whoever was sleeping in Felix's bed at the time.

My sorrow returned. It got so bad that I went back to the doctor to get more medication for my emotional state. But the doctor refused to give me anything when I told her I was still using alcohol. After that, I knew there was a problem, so I dug deep and stopped drinking. I was determined to shake that monkey without any artificial aid. I couldn't believe that I had ended up being the victim again. At least I wasn't homeless that time.

I had no control over what anyone said about me or to me. There were many times when Felix's' friends would walk up to me and ask me why I told his wife about us. No matter what I said, people refused to believe that I didn't care enough about Felix to tell

❖

Dorthea or that she was smart enough to figure it out on her own. Eventually, I stopped responding. I stopped frequenting certain places I might run into them. I was ostracized. It was as if Dorthea, Wanda, and Bonnie had embroidered the scarlet letter on my chest themselves. It didn't make sense to me.

There I was again, left to bear all of the responsibility of what had happened. I was mad at myself for continuing to allow others to suck my soul dry. It wasn't always like that.

Early in life, I realized that I was very sensitive and people took advantage of that. I learned quickly to protect myself and became loud and opinionated. The louder I was the thicker my armor got. As I grew up, I realized that my behavior turned people off and I learned to hold my tongue. But when I did that, I lost the only protection I'd ever had. Having no protection left my soul exposed. I absorbed every negative comment and allowed them to become a part of me.

That experience left me extremely vulnerable. My usual outlets weren't enough and I didn't have alcohol to comfort me anymore. I needed to talk to someone who would listen and remind me of my worth. I had no choice but to call Naja. She had always been there for me, but I hated calling her that time. She had helped me pick up the pieces after I left Antonio and Felix, and I didn't want to admit I had been taken advantage of again.

I got lost in routine. My job required me to be gone many evenings. I escorted the kids in my program on field trips. We went ice-skating, to WNBA games, and performed community service projects. I also taught them life skills, something I found ironic. The activities kept my mind active. I didn't have to

❖

concentrate on my own issues. As usual, I denied myself the opportunity to heal.

Eventually my coat of armor became thick again and I got my protection back. I swore I would never allow anyone to treat me less than I deserved. I had made a conscious effort to repress my feelings of worthlessness so far inside my gut that they would stay lost forever.

It was 3:00 p.m. on August 17, 2001 before I realized I'd turned a year older. Regina reminded me that I was 30-years-old and not getting any younger. She was the only person who remembered. She called and told me to get my shit together because we were going out to celebrate. I wasn't in the mood, but the kids would be back in three weeks, so now was the time to go out and take advantage of it.

She suggested that we go to Cocobongo, the hottest Latin club in Orlando. I convinced her to go to the Bob Marley Café instead because I loved reggae music and didn't feel like standing against the wall while she danced the night away. The only times I showed off my salsa skills were at one of her house parties. You don't go to a salsa club with mediocre moves. And besides, I didn't have salsa heels.

I put on my hip hugger jeans and a red fitted blouse, black wedges and was dressed to impress. The club was really nice. The ceiling opened to the sky, so instead of looking up into fluorescent lights, you looked right at the stars. It was in the middle of August, hot and balmy, so the breeze from the open veranda was great. If you preferred to just hang, you could go upstairs on the patio. But the best part was listening to the 506 Crew perform live.

Reggae penetrates my soul. I love to jam to the sound of the guitar, bass and drums that encompass

❖

reggae music. There's only one problem with reggae: the dance is very seductive. If you dance with a stranger, he invariably gets aroused. If you dance by yourself, you look like a stripper without her pole. You spend all night trying to keep an appropriate distance from guys who have spent the past five songs working up an erection and want to relieve it on you. And if you aren't skilled enough, one will. It's a sick game, but it's fun.

I would've preferred to go to the club with the man I was going home with that night, but since I didn't have one, Regina would have to do. We danced the night away. I worked up a long-needed sweat and released some long-held tension.

The dancing made me feel light, but it wasn't helping my self-esteem. It was true that I hadn't been out dancing in a while, but I was working my stripper moves hard. I couldn't believe no one danced with me. No one asks for a dance at a reggae club. You just find a man behind you, moving to your rhythm. I guess my rhythm needed work too.

We went out for the next two weekends, going back and forth, between salsa for her and reggae for me. We had a great time, but grew tired of compromising. After those couple of weeks, we started meeting up Sunday mornings at our favorite breakfast spot to exchange club stories. Her stories were always more exciting than mine. Sometimes, I didn't even have a story to tell. I would just meet her at the restaurant after a night at home in front of my TV.

I wasn't interested in meeting anyone seriously, but I did meet a couple of guys I thought would be nice to hang out with until the kids came back. There was the cockeyed Puerto Rican who I thought was 19. I didn't always know which eye to look in, but

❖

basically his eyes and age didn't matter. Yes, he was a bit young, but I wasn't trying to marry him. But then I figured out that he was actually a 17-year–old, unemployed high school dropout who was still at home with his mother. I knew something was wrong when every time we talked on the phone he put us on three-way so his best friend could talk, too.

The other guy I met was Sterling. I made his acquaintance at a Kappa Alpha Psi fundraiser. He was short and portly. He was also educated, worked for a large computer company and made more than $200,000 a year. He also played the saxophone and was working on a CD with a few of his fraternity brothers. Finally, a man about something, and he was interested in me!

One evening, he invited me to hang out with his band after they played. I felt honored because only girlfriends and wives did that. Then his phone rang. He politely excused himself and said he needed to take the call. It was from his wife.

Wife?

I knew I wasn't going to find my soul mate at a club, but this was ridiculous.

❖

Track 12

Jaja

With every day that passes,
The feeling in my heart intensifies for you.
Distant memories get me through the lonely times.
I play back phone messages to hear your voice.
Recorded conversations
Capture precious moments shared between us.

I'm missing your touch,
Your smile,
Your generosity of spirit,
Your smell,
Your laughter,
And your kiss.

There is a constant ache
In the foundation of my existence,

A void.
You taught me Jah is puttin me tru nuff test
As I aspire to be nuttin less than the best.
You've set a standard.

I'm missing your touch,
Your smile,
Your generosity of spirit,
Your smell,
Your laughter,
And your kiss.

An inspiration you are,
A mighty, mighty, being you are.
Epitome.
Embodiment.
Quintessence of MAN.
Jaja ... God's gift ... my gift.

I'm missing your touch,
Your smile,
Your generosity of spirit,
Your smell,
Your laughter,
And your kiss.

September came before Noel sent me another email.
He wrote that life was treating us cruelly, trying hard
to keep us apart. He was still in Negril, he said, and
that his job there would last longer than the December
deadline. He told me that he missed our conversations
and would try to get to a computer every two weeks.

It would be more like once a month.

I hoped I could convince him to come back to
the States once the project was over. We missed each

❖

other. Was it my buzzard luck that was making it so difficult for us to connect? It was just another pitiless joke and my misery was the punch line.

I had only so much time to pine for him. Summer was over and my kids were back. They commanded all of my energy. But every so often, yearning thoughts of him would come through. Some image would come on TV or love song would play on the radio and all the longing I had worked so hard to suppress would surge back.

I couldn't control my emotions. I could be on the way to work, or at a friend's house and my feelings would so overwhelm me that I'd burst into tears. I would cry so hard and so long that I looked as if I'd been in a fight. Traumatic childhood memories bubbled to the surface. They would play over and over again, haunting me. I took up a kick boxing class to fill up the few hours of time when I had nothing scheduled.

My thoughts and memories became harder and harder to repress. Everything bothered me. I closed myself off from the world so I didn't have to face it or feel any pain. Noel was the only positive in my life, besides my kids, and I let myself get lost in thoughts of him.

I had begun sharing my poetry with him. I was nervous about it, but still felt it was the right thing to do. He wrote back, saying he loved my poetry and giving me his new cell number. I was on cloud nine.

He also said that he felt like I'd rejected him when he left the States and so had tried not to put his heart in us. That comment made me sick at heart. Had I ruined my chances at a future with him because of the way I behaved before he left? For an entire year after he left, I'd hoped and prayed he'd come back to

❖

me. Meanwhile, he'd tried his best to forget me. Talk about misunderstanding.

On the up side, the new cell number gave me hope that I could hear his voice soon. I was anxious to talk about him returning to the States. But it would be another month before I would hear from him again.

I spent the next couple of months writing more of my thoughts. The poems went from sorrow and despair to love and happiness. They were about Noel and how he made me feel.

We continued to try to connect with each other but our efforts fell short. Once, he went home to Kingston and left the paper with my number on it in Negril. Another time, he called and I missed him. This type of ill luck went on for months. But in December of 2002 things changed. He realized that his new cell phone could send and receive text messages.

We could exchange messages every day – and did.

We spent the next two years nurturing each other spiritually, emotionally and sometimes physically through emails, text messages, instant messages (IMs), phone calls and computer cameras. Our messages ranged from the short "I miss you," to beautiful words of encouragement and three-hour IMs. This man was more than a guardian angel sent to take care of me during a low period. He served a higher purpose. He was my gift from God. I was patient and he was my reward.

Of course, tests were thrown our way and, as buzzard luck would have it, shortly after Noel and I found our rhythm, my computer crashed. I couldn't connect with Noel at all. The waiting was difficult but not like before. The more I wrote, the better I felt. I wasn't as much of a recluse as before, either. I

❖

entertained and went out with friends. Life seemed to be getting back to normal.

Then Antonio called. His mom had told him I was looking for him.

"What's up?" he asked.

He'd been gone two years. To listen to him, you'd think he'd stopped by yesterday. I was furious.

"How dare you," I said. "How dare you call after all this time and say, 'What's up?' The only thing you should be doing is explaining."

He told me the story about his child support problems and I reminded him that I wasn't the one who had a child-support order out against him. I explained that I was most concerned about Kaiya. She had been asking for him. He still refused to give me his phone number or address. I told him that every time he dropped in and out of her life, she would have nightmares. He said nothing.

Before handing the phone to Kaiya, I did tell him that I needed money. I asked him to send anything he could afford. I guess he couldn't afford anything, despite working as a manager in a warehouse where cars were shipped in and out of the country, because I didn't receive a dime.

Noel and I shared many interests, including our desire to connect with our ancestors and reclaim our roots. I learned that "nakupenda" was Swahili for "I love you," and "Malaika" stood for "angel." Of course, I called him Jaja, "God's gift."

During those two years we exhausted all means of contacting one another. I can't count how many emails I sent him. There were many missed phone calls. He called and left a message for me one Valentine's Day, but I missed it. I kept that message for months and played it back at least once a week. I

❖

remember that particular Valentine's Day because I was trying not to stay at home and feel sorry for myself, so I took the kids out to eat. They were my Valentines.

Toward the end of March of 2003, I happened to see that Noel was online. I was thrilled. He told me that he was back home from work for the weekend to see Louis Farrakhan speak in Kingston. We talked until it was time for him to leave.

Noel and I talked about everything. I told him that I wanted to visit him but he said his schedule was too hectic. He wouldn't be able to spend the quality time with me that he wanted. I had to continue to settle for being pen pals.

I sent Noel a care package for his birthday in November. It contained candles, shower gel, and books. He never let anyone touch the candles and told me that every time he lighted them he saw and felt us together. He really knew how to make me feel good. He said that whenever he used the shower gel, he could feel my silky caress on his body. He was spreading it on thick, but it was exactly what I needed hear. He told me that he carried pictures of me in his wallet and that he longed for my touch as much as I did his, but that we needed to be strong.

He'd reread all of my emails. He felt that I was putting him on a pedestal and that he didn't deserve that. I heard that from him so often that I started to wonder whether there was something he wasn't telling me. But I ignored my gut instinct. I reminded him of the times he went out of his way for me.

After fifteen minutes of expressing our undying love for each other, we caught up on old times. We talked about everything as if we had been best friends forever.

❖

It was so easy to talk to him. Some of our best conversations were when he would try to seduce me. He would tell me how he wished he were right there behind me while I typed, nibbling on my ear and my neck. He would go into much detail about how he would slip his hands under my blouse, gently run them up to my breasts, circle my nipples, and watch them grow taut and erect with each flick of his tongue.

I would just sit there and drift into deep thought while he talked about what he was going to do to me. Then he would ask me to continue. I wasn't as good at cyber sex as he was. He would always tell me to slow down. It was fun but a bit too much pressure for me. I didn't know what to say or when to say it. He could go on for hours. I wanted to tell him that I didn't need all that foreplay and to just give me mine right then, right there.

We reminisced about our few but special moments together, especially our first night together. We laughed about my roommate and wished we'd had more memories together at the park. When I got anxious about seeing him, he told me to close my eyes and "create more memories" of us. He had no idea that I was already doing that. I pictured him in the park, at my house and in my bed. Noel spoke like a beautifully written romance novel and I loved it.

I told him that I dreamed of finding someone who made me feel the way he did: cherished, secure, wanted, and needed. Sometimes he would slip into patois.

"Fi real; dem sinting de yu fi get yes! "

"Please translate."

"Those things are what you ought to get of course."

I was trying my best to figure out how to get it.

❖

"Jah is puttin us tru nuff test. Settle for nuttin less den de best."

He had no idea how many tests I'd already endured and failed. How many more would there be? I didn't trust men, or maybe I didn't trust myself not take to be taken advantage of. I knew that I was a work in progress, but I made a conscious decision to keep that from him. I didn't want him to know that part of me. I would get myself together. By the time he returned to me, I would be okay.

It was Carnival time in Jamaica, so the entire island was in party mode. He was still traveling back in forth to Negril for work and he commented about the tourists on the island partaking in hedonistic activities. He didn't usually join in the carnival festivities because people became too uninhibited. He had gone to one pool party and spent most of the time watching adults drink too much and lose all their virtue and good sense. He compared it to the big celebrations mentioned in the worshiping of the golden calf and other religious celebrations in which our people went astray.

That conversation made me uncomfortable, considering my behavior during Orlando's Carnival a couple of years prior. Misunderstanding my silence, he said he must have sounded like a bore. All I could think of was what I would sound like if I told him my Carnival experience.

I did tell him that I enjoyed going to Carnival because I loved to dance. He loved to dance as well and boasted that he could break anybody down on the dance floor.

He said he couldn't help but wonder if I were the one for him and regret that he'd let the chance slip away. I told him to keep his heart open to the

❖

possibilities. It upset me that he sounded as if he'd given up on the idea of us. He assured me he had not, but said he wasn't going to let his emotions get the better of him. Then he suggested that we have some form of courtship to know what we were really feeling.

He had a great sense of humor and even though he suggested that we court, he also joked that we needed a shrink for carrying on a relationship online. He had no idea how true that statement was for me. He asked me what it was about me that burned him up inside, left him anxiety filled, and feeling like life stood still.

For me there was no doubt it was our spiritual connection. Ours wasn't just a chance meeting. My car had stopped so that I could meet him and experience the kindness of a real man. I needed him at that very moment. He was sent to me because of God's grace. He often told me that he was grateful for being able to have impacted my life in such positive ways.

❖

Track 13

Love Story

Love, Love, Love
Love, Love, Love

This is my love story.
I wouldn't change a word.
I can't wait to turn the pages
To read another word
Of how you make me feel.
It keeps me excited
About what my life can be.
I dream of you every night
And can't wait to rise again
To get to the next chapter
Of this story for me to live.

Love, Love, Love
Love, Love, Love

This is my love story.
When I read the words on the page
I hope this feeling never ends.
Chapter seven is my favorite.
I can read it again and again.
That's when our worlds met,
And my love story really began.
Whenever I put the book down,
And we're apart,
I keep the memories close to me.
Tucked deep inside my heart.

Love, Love, Love
Love, Love, Love

This is my love story.
I read it every day.
How we wake up together,
Each and every day;
How your breath feels against my neck,
And your touch feels on my skin.
I won't put this book down for another,
No matter how it ends,
Because I know I will never have this feeling
With anyone else again.

We made dates to meet online or by phone on a
regular basis. Our conversations always lasted a few
hours, and the time I spent waiting for him seemed
like hours, too. He would be tired after travel for
hours from the country, but he always called or signed
on because he knew I was waiting. We started just

❖

about every conversation the same way. I'd ask him if he were tired and he'd say yes, but he knew that I'd be waiting.

He was interested in everything about me and never failed to ask me what was going on in my life. He was so very different from Felix, who never asked. The only subjects Felix and I talked about were his broken knees, his headaches, his bad back or the sorry co-workers that he worked with.

I only told Noel the good stuff about me because I was afraid to let him know the real me. I feared he would find out how much of a failure I was, how unlovable I was. I created the person Noel got to know. I tried to impress him with my strength, creativity, and entrepreneurial spirit. He had no idea how much of an emotional cripple I was, how I struggled with self-esteem, or how alone I felt. I was convinced that if he found out the person I was he would leave me, too. I worked hard to make him come back to me because he was the only person who genuinely cared and gave me the attention I desired.

When I looked at my life, what did I have to be proud of? In short, my kids. They excelled in sports and the arts: Kaiya and Tariq were into Tae Kwan Do. Kaiya excelled in soccer and basketball and Tariq was a fantastic artist with lots of friends. They were well-mannered, outstanding students. They were my greatest accomplishments, so I talked about them most often.

Discussions about my children inevitably led to thoughts about my dream of establishing the Angel's Village Community Center. Noel inspired me to begin work on a business plan for the center. It was hard but I got it done. I spent months doing research and attending seminars given by the Small Business

❖

Administration, looking into loans, filing for my non-profit status, and vetting locations. I was both inspired and overwhelmed. I did ask one guy to help me but he charged me more than I could handle so I let him go. It was more stress than I'd expected. Things weren't going according to my timeline. I grew increasingly worried and uncertain that I could plan the business on my own. Noel was there for me to confide in.

Sex often crept into our conversations, even when we were talking about something as unrelated as the community center.

"What's taking you off your timeline?" he'd ask, and then sneak in, "What's stopping you from the climax?"

While I was still getting over that first line, he'd say something like, "The first time will always give you the jitters, just like with sex."

Noel was extremely intellectual and spiritual. He introduced me to so many alternative ideas and readings and made me think about matters that I otherwise would've felt were outside my comfort zone or wouldn't have been exposed to. I was open to his ideas because he wasn't arrogant or condescending. He encouraged me to come to my own conclusions. He made me think and that was a change from any relationship I'd ever had. He was also willing to admit that he didn't have all the answers and that he was in search of the truth himself, so we searched together.

He told me that Farrakhan was as great as expected but that it was more of an inspiring speech for him, rather than a lesson.

He shared some of Farrakhan's quotes about women and I really liked them:

"Educate a man, you have educated an

❖

individual, educate a woman and you've educated a nation. "

"If there is such a thing as a no-good woman, look close by you'll find a no-good man encouraging her to be that way."

"Look at a man, you see a God. But look at a woman and you'll see the creator of a God."

I thought about how my ex-husband had left the country to keep from paying child support and how his girlfriend and his mother protected him. His mother wouldn't even tell me where he was. Those were two no-good women protecting that no-good man.

Noel and I would reference not only the Bible, but also the Qur'an. We'd talk about Buddhism, Hinduism, and more alternative religious beliefs, like Kemetism and the Ausar Auset Society.

He was as excited to talk to me as I was to talk to him. He used to tell me that I wiped the sleep away. He always ended all of our conversations with the words, "Nakupenda, Malaika."

The next time I saw Noel online he'd been on for about twenty minutes. He wouldn't respond to my IMs and I was getting really irritated, especially since we were supposed to meet at 8 a.m. When I got on at the appointed time, I found a message telling me to meet him at 9:30 a.m. because he felt tired. I went back on at 9:30 and he still wasn't there. I waited and then finally wrote that I hoped he'd have time at 11. If not, we'd talk when we talked. At 11 a.m., I was still on, waiting for him, and he wouldn't respond to me.

All of a sudden, I heard that digital door shut, signaling that Noel had signed off. I sent him a text

❖

message to his phone, telling him how rude it was and how it was as though he'd slammed the door in my face.

He signed right back on and said he hadn't realized that I was waiting for him. His mom was using his sign-on to do research for his father and he'd left the house.

"But I've been waiting for you since eight," I said.

He told me that he was sure he'd signed on at 9:37 a.m. because he set his alarm clock for 9:25 and took ten minutes to freshen up.

I continued fussing and he finally interrupted me to apologize for the misunderstanding.

He cut me off as respectfully as a gentleman could and asked me how I was doing. I was relieved when he changed the subject because I was really upset, and I would've beat that dead horse into the ground. Had I just let him in on my crazy tendencies? I wondered.

He told me to keep typing because he was printing some things off for his father and that he would play catch up. Apparently, his grandfather's potassium was so high that the doctors weren't sure why his heart hadn't stopped. I really felt foolish.

I typed random thoughts for about five minutes about any and everything before he finally joined in. I mentioned that I was having really vivid dreams about us. These dreams were extremely intense. Sometimes they would wake me out of a sound sleep. They felt so real.

I also rambled on about teaching the kids at the Village House about mutual respect, because the kids didn't seem to have any. I had to stop a fight between so-called best friends after one disrespected the

❖

other.

"Here in every day life we are quite mindful of the elderly," Noel wrote. He wished that everyone acted that way.

Noel had no idea how he spoke my life with his words. I had a real problem with letting just anyone into my life. I would make that the topic of my next lesson for the kids: Get to know people before you fully let them in. Sounded like great advice.

I responded by saying, "I don't know why people treat me the way they do."

Noel told me several times that I was too nice.

He also told me that growth came from the continued ability to stimulate your mind to seek truth, wisdom, knowledge, and "overstanding."

"Overstanding?" I repeated.

He said I felt taken advantage of because I was dealing with people who were still in a state of "downpression" and didn't even realize it. We all just need to come together in an organized manner and let our visions be seen by all. From there, all those who have ears to hear will hear, and eyes to see will see.

"Downpression?"

"If you are understanding, you can't possibly comprehend yourself, and if you are oppressing, you can't lift the people up!"

I had to reflect on that.

He pressed me about my dream about him and I told every juicy detail. Sometimes I thought he was actually next to me when I slept. The dreams were frustrating, especially when they woke me up out of a sound sleep. They were mostly sexual, sometimes nice and sweet, but mainly animalistic.

I went on and on and didn't leave out any details of my dream. I included everything, from what

I was wearing, to what perfume I had on and the sounds we made. I must have created a nice picture, because I finally got my invitation to Jamaica. He made it clear that he wouldn't be able to see me all the time but that he would make as much time for me as he could.

He didn't have a choice after I told him about that dream. He said he couldn't wait for us to walk, talk, wine and dine, and make the most fantastic and explosive love ever. I couldn't wait, either. That's what I was waiting to hear. I worked hard for that invite and made him think it was his idea. I made sure to ask if he were seeing anyone. Thank goodness, he said he wasn't.

By then he was in Montego Bay, working on a new project, and needed to settle in to his new site before I went down. A week later, he sent me an email telling me his grandpa had passed away. I wished I could've been there to comfort him, but couldn't be.

❖

Track 14

I Live In My Dreams

Today, when I awakened,
I had to clutch my heart,
For I felt you right here with me,
Even though we're apart.
I could almost feel you holding me,
My heart began to race,
As I thought of how you kiss me,
And how you touch my face.
I want to scream and tell the world
Of the love I feel for you,
But I must love in silence.
That is all that I can do.
Who can I tell?
What would they say?

Could they understand?
"You know that's not really your man."
You're there and I am here. No one understands.
Whether it's right,
Or whether it's wrong,
Let the truth be told.
I no longer love you with just my heart;
I love you with my soul.

After more than three long years, in June 2003, I finally got to see Jaja. I was going to win his heart once and for all. My cousin, Veeshous, who lived in Miami, went to Kingston with me to visit a friend of hers. I rented a car and drove down from Orlando at about 4:00 that morning. It was insane. I hadn't slept at all because I'd been running around in Orlando the night before and online with Noel until about 2:30 that morning.

I had a hard time staying awake during that lonely, smoke-filled drive down I-95 South. Florida was so hot that spontaneous brush fires burned on both sides of the highway. I blasted the radio, sang at the top of my lungs and drank lots of coffee to stay awake. It smelled like burnt wood that entire summer.

My cousin had some running around to do in Miami before our flight took off and of course we got to Miami International Airport a little later than we should have. We dropped the car off at the rental office. By the time we got to check-in, the line it was at least two hours long.

Once we realized that we were still forty-five minutes away from reaching the counter but had only fifteen minutes before our flight took off, my cousin pleaded to be let through the line. The ticket agent

❖

told us that there was no way and that we would never make the fight. They obviously weren't used to dealing with my fast talking-cousin because the next thing I knew we were ducking under the ropes to check-in. With ten minutes to spare, the ticket agent informed my cousin that she needed to either pay extra or put her baggage in lockers because she had too much. She decided not pay the extra fair, so we ran to the other side of the ticket counter to store her baggage.

By then I was an emotional wreck. I prayed that we didn't miss that flight. It was a scene out of one of those Hertz commercials when O.J. ran through the terminal and over counters. The gate was in front of us, about two hundred meters away, when they made the last boarding call. We screamed for them to hold the door. I was surprised security didn't stop us with all the noise we made.

For a moment there, it seemed as though we were going to make it. But then, with me being Public Enemy No. 1, security stopped me at the door for an additional search. They pulled me to the side, checked my carry-on bag, and waved a wand under my skirt to make sure I didn't have anything suspicious. Thank goodness, I'd put the items I bought from the adult accessory store in my checked luggage. Having security see that stuff would have been embarrassing.

With two minutes to spare, I boarded that plane to Kingston to get my future husband.

The flight took only a few hours, but I found it unbearably long. I was delirious with lack of sleep, but too excited to even close my eyes. I thought I'd keep my mind busy by identifying the islands below, but the only island we passed over was Cuba. I would've ordered a rum punch, but I was scared I'd get off the plane wasted and embarrass myself in front of Noel.

❖

When we arrived at Kingston's tiny airport, friendly greeters welcomed us to the island. Everyone sang. I was embarrassed to be so openly excited, but couldn't help myself. I giggled and waved back at the greeters. I felt like I'd just won a spot on the Price Is Right.

I walked outside the doors of the airport, expecting Noel to be waiting for my cousin, Veeshous, and me to take us to the hotel, but he wasn't. I walked back and forth, noting all the other guys who were waiting for someone to get off the plane. Onlookers filled both sides of the walkway. I felt a little self-conscious. Strange eyes stared back at me and squinted because of the sun. That wiped the smile right off my face. Kingston was no resort town.

I would have passed Noel if he had not stepped out from the crowd. He wore dark sunglasses and didn't smile either. I tried to maintain my composure while he walked toward me. I was calm until I was a few feet away and then I couldn't take it anymore. I dropped my luggage, threw my arms up, and leaped into his arms. He flashed that beautiful smile and sang my name. It felt so good to finally be in his arms again. I melted against him and tried to hold on to that moment for as long as I could.

I spent four days and three nights in Kingston. We walked and talked, wined and dined, and spent hours in the Caribbean Sea, just like he said we would. He cooked me breakfast and took it to the hotel. He prepared plantain, callaloo, fried dumplings, and ackee, a white fleshy fruit that contains a toxin and can kill you if not prepared correctly. It resembles scrambled eggs when cooked. He took me to his home and introduced me to his mother. Then, he and I walked around his yard, which was as large as a fruit

❖

grove. I recalled the strolls we took under the weeping willows in Orlando.

The yard had so many wonderful trees: breadfruit, banana, coconut, and mango. His mom grew lots of orchids, as well. Fifteen or so dogs roamed the yard. Noel said they were for security. Between the dogs and the cacti that lined the perimeter of the house, he had no problems with intruders.

We went to a secluded beach where food was cooked under thatched roofed huts. After we parked the car, Noel walked over to a guy who hung out in the parking lot and gave him some cash. The graveled area where we parked didn't look like it was the kind of establishment where you had to pay.

"Why'd you slip him money?" I asked.

"So he'll make sure no one messes with the car."

What a hustle! I wish I could stand out in front of Walmart and have people give me protection money.

That afternoon was magical. We spent hours in the cold water, keeping warm in each other's arms. We asked strangers to take pictures of us hugging under the palm trees and had a romantic moonlit dinner under the hut.

He drove me out to the country, where I met his grandmother and other friends and family. On our way there I took pictures of the cows that walked along the side of the road. They were so close I could've reached out and touched them. It was awesome!

When he wasn't around, I explored Kingston on foot. The heat billowed off the concrete. People waited at the bus stop and the Kentucky Fried

❖

Chicken on the corner, shuffling impatiently and fanning against the heat. Kingston reminded me of where I'd grown up in St. Louis. The only difference was being unable to understand what people were saying, except for the occasional 'Ya, mon.'

When Noel returned to the hotel, I told him about my explorations. He looked at me as though I was crazy and told me I was brave. I had no idea that I was in so much danger. Ignorance is bliss.

Of course, we did the Ooo-we! That goes without saying. I played a CD with some of my favorite songs and it played in the background while we got to know each other again. It had songs like "Tonight is the Night," by Betty Wright, and "Let's Get it On," by Marvin Gay. I bought lots of tea lights and floated them in water and we made good use of my massage oil. I tried to recreate that romantic evening we had on our first date, but it wasn't like the first time at all. Instead of holding my head gently in his hands, he laid Kingston down. I didn't see fireworks; I felt pipe bombs. I just held on for dear life. It was shock and awe.

Then it was over, time to return to reality.

On the way to the airport, we stopped off at a flea market so I could spend the rest of my money. I bought souvenirs for the kids and sandals for myself. Noel bought me a nice hand-carved wall hanging that depicted a couple smooching under a palm tree. I still had some cash remaining and tried to give it to him, but he refused it.

"But what am I going to do with it?" I asked.

"Spend it when you come back."

When we arrived at the airport I was determined not to have a good-bye that was even close to the last one we had. When he offered to drop me off

❖

at the parking lot I refused. I insisted that he park and walk me to the door. I held him tight and kissed him as much as I could. If I could've stayed, I would have.

When it was time to board the plane, I walked away slowly, hoping that he would run up behind me, grab my arm, spin me around and tell me that he couldn't spend another day without me. But he didn't.

When I arrived back home, I got stranded in Miami because of bad planning. I had no one to pick me up, so I had to take a train up the next day, and then I had no choice but to call Felix to pick me up from the station.

Instead of driving me directly home, he drove me around to two different work sites. He reminded me of me when Antonio came to visit me in college. He made sure all of his friends saw me in his car. The same guys who were pissed at me for "telling" Felix's wife huddled around the car like we were old friends again. He told everyone how I had just come back from Jamaica and how I had gotten my groove back. He laughed hysterically. I didn't find anything funny. Why couldn't he just take me home? There was no point in what he was trying to do. I'll never understand men.

I saw Noel online a couple of days later. He made sure to tell me immediately that his mom was online and that he'd catch me later. That was funny. I'll bet his mom saw me come online and yelled to Noel, "That crazy be-yatch is online." I pictured Noel running through the hall, jumping over furniture to let me know he was not the one online so I wouldn't say something stupid to his mamma again. The memory of how I'd behaved embarrassed me.

He came online about twenty minutes later and we reminisced about our weekend together. I was

❖

ready and waiting for him to confess his undying love for me and ask me to move to Jamaica. He didn't. Instead, he talked about how he'd been reading Marcus Garvey's Life & Lessons. He asked how my kids liked their souvenirs. He told me how I warmed his heart while we held each other at the beach, but said nothing about being in love with me, or wanting to spend the rest of his life with me.

When I told him that I appreciated his hospitality and how wonderful he was, he said he was humbled by the magnitude of my love, and that he didn't deserve all that I said about him. Then he said he was sleepy and needed to go to bed.

I hadn't been eating or sleeping well. I felt uneasy but couldn't say why. The last time I'd had that feeling was when I'd taken a weekend trip to Paris with Mom and found out that my ex-husband was sleeping with yet another girl. My gut talked to me even though I didn't always listen. Something was up with Noel. I could sense it.

The next time we talked, he said his cousin, who was only thirty-eight, had passed away and that his grandmother had been rushed to the hospital two weeks prior with terrible stomach pains. She was very weak and her stool was black and extra smelly because of internal bleeding. The doctors had cleaned her out and given her a blood transfusion. Taking aspirin and other prescription drugs at the same time caused her bleeding. Maybe that was why I'd been feeling uneasy. Maybe we were so close I could feel his pain.

❖

Track 15

His Grace

Constantly amid thought,
You as subject,
I quietly yearn,
With a fever-like burn,
On an eternal search,
Blissful is the way,
I feel about my devotion
To you.
My thoughts don't stay hushed
I surrender,
Defeated.
I let down my guard
To a powerful force.
And kneel before the alter of truth,
And I call upon the Almighty,

"Continue to sanctify me with water for my mind,
control for my body,
And an escort for my soul."
Every second 'pon minute,
Minute 'pon hour,
Hour 'pon day,
I gain a bit more clarity,
And understanding for my journey.
I'm in no doubt of my tomorrow.
Because my today was guided,
Never walked alone,
Led with understanding,
Mercy, and grace.

Lightning zapped my computer during a storm in August in the middle of the rainy season. Florida has daily downpours from May to October. You can almost time them to the half hour. I saw the lightening, but paid it no mind. I didn't realize that my power strip didn't offer surge protection. There was a crackle, then a pop and a puff of smoke. I knew immediately what had happened.

I snuck online at work, at my cousin's house, and anywhere else I could to try to talk to Noel. It was mid-October when I finally caught up with him and Jamaica's general elections had just taken place. He said the voting had been relatively peaceful, "with only ten, maybe fifteen murders," and that he'd been busy helping friends repair doors broken by the opposition when it tried to force its way into people's houses.

It was one thing hearing about this kind of violence on the news and quite another to hear about it from someone I knew. All I could think about was Noel's safety. I couldn't stand not being able to communicate with him whenever I wanted to, so I invested in a computer I couldn't afford.

Noel had experienced more death in his family in the last two years than I had since being a child. Thomas was going down, so I gave him a care package for Noel. I was still working hard to make him mine, even though it didn't seem to be working. We expressed our love for each other often, but he never mentioned coming to the States and he certainly didn't mention me joining him in Jamaica.

One day, there was an unexpected knock at my door. I looked through the sliding glass window so they wouldn't see me. Oh my goodness! Look what the dog drug to my door: Old Tricky Felix in the flesh.

What was he doing here? I started not to open the door, but curiosity got the best of me. He greeted me with his usual, 'Good afternoon, Ms. Lady.'

Except for when he'd picked me up at the airport, it had been more than a year since I'd seen that serpent. The last time was when he was telling his wife that I didn't mean anything to him and that I was just "something to do."

I tried not to let my confusion show, but he must've seen it on my face. I didn't ask him in quick enough, because he asked to be invited in. I stepped back and let him in, still having not said a word.

He should've called before stopping by. Didn't he realize that he'd lost the privilege of coming over without an invitation a long time ago? Didn't he care? Obviously not, because here he was, in all his glory, with that same simple grin.

An intense rage overcame me. I fantasized about drop kicking him in his knees so I could watch him grimace in pain. I wanted to trade his silly grin for all the pain he'd caused me. Instead, I waited to

❖

hear what he had to say.

He took a few steps inside and closed the door behind him. The last time he showed up unexpectedly was to tell me his wife had snuck up on him. What had happened now? Why did he think I'd care?

"I've been going to church," he said.

"What does that have to do with me?"

Then he asked me for my forgiveness. I couldn't believe it. He was serious. Maybe he wasn't the devil after all. I repressed a smile. For once, someone thought enough about me to care about my feelings. I opened my mouth, ready to speak, but he beat me to it.

He looked me right in the eye and said, "Of course, I don't care if you do or don't forgive me, because I've forgiven myself."

That snatched all the wind out of me. I felt as though he'd punched me in my gut. I'd let him beat me to the smack down again. His visit had nothing to do with spiritual cleansing. He'd driven seven miles out of his way to gloat. He was evil, an agent working for the devil. Lucifer himself had possessed Felix's body and was directing it to undo a year's worth of my healing.

"I know you called immigration," he said.

Those heifers! I cussed them out under my breath, especially Bonnie. She was so concerned about her husband not finding out that she'd had anything to do with it. I knew we weren't friends, but to tell on me was ridiculous.

Felix went on to tell me how stressed out he'd been and how he hadn't slept, not knowing when he would be deported. His "friends" hadn't bothered to tell him that immigration wasn't going to do anything because he wasn't involved in any illegal activities.

❖

No wonder everyone had abandoned me. Those women had ignored their own part and blamed me for everything. In a sense, I'd made it easy for them to do it: After all, I hadn't run around town, telling who was involved or defending myself. I'd made myself a convenient scapegoat. I was a Hester Prynne, not in the puritanical Boston of the 1700s but the hedonistic Orlando of 2003.

I wouldn't stand for it anymore. I told Felix the whole story. I didn't feel I owed him anything or that he deserved any explanation, but I was pissed at those bitches. Hell, I was pissed at everybody.

Disillusionment and hurt crossed his face after I'd spilled my guts. I knew that look very well because I saw it every time I looked in the mirror. He said something about them pretending to be his friends. What a joke! They were all two-faced assholes, including Felix. He couldn't wait to tell Clyde what Bonnie had done because he knew how upset he would be. I laughed under my breath because I wanted to tell him what Clyde and I had done.

He rambled on about his troubles over the past year. Just as I was recovering from that gut punch, he delivered another virtual blow. There were ways to get the immigration thing behind him, he said. Rufus thought that I was so in love with him that I would marry him, he said, and then looked at me, as if to ask, Do you understand?

I understood all right. I just couldn't believe what that jerk had just said to me. Felix did have a big mouth but I didn't think he was that stupid. He didn't even try to sweet talk me. I pictured him and Rufus at the office after work, sharing a bottle of Royal Oak. Godfather Rufus had leaned back in his chair with one hand on his potbelly and laughed about how easy it

❖

would be to take advantage of me.

I did believe in Karma, but I wanted to affect his future existence on my terms. Because I didn't say no, he felt comfortable and took a seat on the couch. He talked about a whole lot of nothing for another hour and then jumped on my computer to check his email. My instant messenger stayed on, especially since I was communicating with Noel on a regular basis again.

About fifteen minutes into Felix's computer use, I heard that rickety door sound, signifying that someone on my buddy list had signed on. A message popped up and Felix put my status on invisible. I stood up to see who had messaged me. It was Noel. I interrupted Felix to respond to Noel's IM. I let him know that someone else was using my computer and that I would be with him soon. Felix took the hint. He stayed online for only another few minutes, and then left. Once he was gone, I jumped on the Internet to talk to my Jaja.

He was such a spiritual person and that grounded me. I felt calm, had no worries and felt no stress when we spoke. His spirit was consistent and I needed him after that brush with Lucifer.

Noel told me that since his grandma had gotten out of the hospital he'd been rubbing her legs with the massage oil that I'd left him. He tried to take her for a walk, but she just wasn't having it. After I left the oil with him, I realized that someone would need to apply it. So I left explicit instructions to rub ONLY his granny's legs down. Whether she was the only one to enjoy the rub down, I didn't know, but I was certainly not going to ask.

I knew I didn't really have him and that it would be just a matter of time before he got bored

❖

with all of it and would need something more. I couldn't hold back my emotions. I let out a sorrowful cry. I felt like Florida Evans when the death of her husband finally sank in. Damn!!!!!!!!! Damn!!!!!!!! Damn!!!!!!!

Later that evening, Bonnie called me to say she "knew" that Felix and I were together again. She sounded disgusted. When Felix left my house, he couldn't wait to go run his mouth and, as usual, it was a load of crap. I tried to tell her that we weren't together but she didn't believe me. She thought I was a dumb home wrecker who couldn't leave Felix alone.

For the next few weeks, Noel and I barely spoke during our time online because I had gotten my camera to work. I did whatever he wanted me to, and what he wanted had nothing to do with speaking.

❖

Committed

We once shared a place
That was ours alone,
A place that was peaceful,
Where our hearts could roam.
We spoke with our eyes,
And touched with our souls.
We shared all we had,
No secrets untold.
We'd sit on the beach,
And watch the sunset.
We'd recount all our joys,
And the day we met.
So good it was,
Then apprehensions so few,
Devotion was plentiful,
Ecstasy anew.

Your thoughts were my thoughts,
And my happiness was yours.
Our problems were not walls,
Merely unopened doors,
You know I never meant to hurt you,
Never meant to make you sad.
But I'm committed to another.
I guess I took for granted,
All the goodness you had.
How if just once more
I could to rest my face in your hands.
You'd read my eyes,
And again you'd understand
How much you really mean to me.

Love Jaja

I don't know why but all of a sudden I hadn't been able to connect with Noel for our long conversations. I still sent him poems; he still sent me text messages from his phone, but there was no real conversation. When we finally connected, in early December of 2003, I scolded him for making me wait so long to hear from him.

I must have been rambling on because I didn't realize he'd asked me how I was doing, so he asked me again. I took a moment before I answered. I got that weird vibe again. He told me that his grandma was back in her home in the country and his mom was in Orlando. He said he missed our conversations and hearing my brilliant laughter, how it was like light piercing clouds on a rainy day. He always knew what to say to me. But there was something in his undertone; that tickle in my gut wouldn't go away.

❖

"Life can be complicated at times, hmm?" he said.

"Yep."

"Seemingly cruel even."

I wasn't quite sure what he was getting at and assumed he was venting. Sometimes, he worked fourteen days straight and was so overwhelmed with fatigue that he wanted to do nothing but sleep. I wished he could collapse in my arms after his long days at work.

I told him about the dream I'd had that morning. It wasn't as exciting as the other dreams I had about him. I dreamed that we spoke on the phone. There was no romance, no excitement. It seemed so real and I woke up from it very sad.
There was a pause before he responded. I wondered if we'd gotten booted offline because he took so long to respond.

"Are you still there?" I asked. "Is something on your mind?"

"There goes that sense of perception you've always had. Yep, I'm still here. I'm just not liking the thought or feeling of having you in limbo, while I'm here trying to sort myself out. It seems cruel and unfair, but at the same time I'm so afraid of losing a chance at life with you. Honestly, I think about you all the time. But the fact that I've committed myself makes me feel obligated to try to see if this will work."

"What are you saying?"

"It's like I've already passed the half-line. "

"Jaja, I can't imagine myself with anyone else. I go to bed every night yearning for you. I wake up every morning yearning for you. My kids are great. Everything is great, but I am missing the icing on my

❖

cake. I like icing. I miss icing. And what does half-line mean?"

"It means that I've already met, said and done too much to just walk away without first trying."

"Trying what?" I asked.

"When you came here and I really realized how committed you were willing to be, it rocked me to the core."

I took a deep breath and typed, "It scares me that you are giving up on us, but at the same time if it's not what you really want, then it wouldn't work regardless of what I feel. I can handle that. Above all else, your friendship is most important."

I was lying through my teeth. I felt like scratching his eyeballs out. At the same time, I wished I were there so I could drop to his feet and beg him to stay with me.

"Knowing that I really wanted to try when we first met and that now, when the opportunity presents itself, I can't just jump at it is a hard pill to swallow," he wrote. "Life and timing can be so mean, especially to those who don't deserve it."

I frowned. "I have only been gone from Jamaica for a few months or so. What happened?"

Then I understood. There was someone else. There had to be. And now he'd chosen between us. I felt sick to my stomach. If I'd known my trip to Jamaica was Sitting Bull's last fight, I would have fought to the death.

"Our friendship has become invaluable," he said. "It's definitely one to cherish and nurture through our journeys. One thing I know is that what's meant to be will be and cannot be stopped by the deeds of man."

❖

"I think about the force that brought you into my life every day. You are such an inspiration to me and I really want my kids to get a chance to experience such a great man's presence."

"Ayo, you are a true queen, with such a calm, soothing spirit. You always deliver such kind expressions. It's just impossible to resist you. It's truly a blessing having you in my life."

Yep, that's me. Always making it easy for other people even when I'm being shat upon. I didn't want to hear anymore of that philosophical crap! No wonder he hadn't been around. He'd been cheating on me! I wanted to scream at the top of my lungs and cuss the hell out of him, but I didn't know how.

"I have been so anxious to show you that I would make a great partner for you," I said. "I have so much love to give. The nurturer in me is desperate for someone to nurture the way a woman nurtures a man."

"You've shown me that the virtuous woman mentioned in the Bible, who is so hard to find, really does exist. I can feel the presence of that furnace of intense love, passion, just waiting to explode and pour it on. But I just can't let this go. Yet it's almost stifling."

"I'll miss receiving in return what I give to you."

"The wrong person won't know how to deal with it. Only abuse it."

This was the story of my life. I had hoped that this time it would be different. He knew that I'd endured so much disappointment. If he cared, then why wasn't he willing to protect me from more of the same? I couldn't believe I was going through that again.

❖

"You have been the only person to give me any type of nurturing," I typed.

"Since the one time I've been really hurt, I have tried hiding and denying what I have to give for fear of it being wasted. This is why I'm so fearful, because you bring it to the surface."

Did he just say "the one time" he'd been hurt. One time? Puh-leeeeeze!

"I've never really allowed myself to go beyond a point where it would be too difficult for me to move on. I usually give time to see what a person is up to before deciding if I stay or go," he wrote.

Okay, so now he was telling me that this wasn't difficult for him. He'd checked me out and decided to go.

"I forgot that I was supposed to meet a bredren from 10:30," he wrote. "He just called my cell. Can we be on for an earlier time tomorrow, say 6:30, 7 p.m.?" Bredren, huh? He was going to be with the one he was committed to.

I didn't speak or see Noel online for another month. When I did, he greeted me as if we'd just spoken yesterday and not as if he'd broken my heart.

"Hello, baby! Could this be true? Am I actually seeing my babe online?"

What is it with men? But I was happy to hear from him, so I responded as though he hadn't broken my heart. I was grinning from ear to ear. He told me that he'd tried to catch me online earlier that day but missed me and tried my cell. My cell wasn't on. The bill came and I ignored it so the "man" decided to turn it off.

I missed him so much. I told him that I loved him and that I couldn't stop thinking about him. I put it out there. A part of me hoped he wanted to talk to

❖

me because he realized that he'd made a big mistake and now wanted me back.

He told me that I'd held a special place in his heart from the day he met me and that the territory had only gotten wider with time. Then he said that the only thing that had stopped him from really saying, "Malaika, I want to be with you. Let's make a try," is that he was committed.

That hadn't gone quite the way I wanted. I didn't mean to get dumped again. He continued to type but I was stuck on those last words. I nearly swallowed my tongue. My love story had just ended like an episode of the Young and the Restless.

"My feelings for you are real," he typed, "and they're difficult to push aside."

I stared at the screen, unable to move.

"'I don't know what to do," he wrote, "but to leave things in the hands of Our Father. He'll light the path and show the way. I trust Him."

Finally, I responded.

"Yes, He will, but sometimes you just have to know when to say when. I mean, you're not in a committed relationship expecting it to end, Jaja. The path is lit."

He didn't respond. Now, we were both staring at our computer screens. Neither of us typed anything for about five minutes. Then he broke the silence.

"Crazy thoughts come into my mind at times, I think about the good times we've had together and I really do miss them. There can be a little strain here at times, but these occur in relationships, and it's just too young a relationship to tell."

I'd been defeated and hadn't even gotten the chance to concede.

❖

With trembling fingers, I typed, "I guess it would be silly for me to say, 'I'll wait for you, but not forever.'"

It was a lie. I would've waited for that man for the rest of my life. I loved him with everything I had. He'd relit a spark that life and hard times had threatened to extinguish.

Feeling as though the air had been sucked from my lungs, I told him to "just be happy." I tried to sound mature, but I so wished I could've been there with him, that he could've seen my face. I would've dropped to my knees and wept.

Slowly, I typed: "I know I said that I hope that we can always be friends, but I really think that would just add salt to the wound."

"I need your friendship," he wrote back.

"And I need your love."

"Words can't express my feelings at this point; I wish I were there by you now. I am sorry to be causing you grief. I feel like a failure, I'm so confused. Why do things have to be the way they are? Please allow me to be a part of the kids' lives as well. I would love to be able to interact with them, just as I need to share with you. Don't cut me off. I won't be salt to any wound."

That was strange to read. It made his leaving even more devastating. I'd never had anyone want either my kids or me in their lives that much. When I left Antonio, he didn't say anything about losing his daughter, and Felix used to ask me why I didn't give Tariq back to his mother.

"I've had so many dreams of teaching them things about life," Noel continued. "I guess we need time, but never close the door to communication."

"I don't need time. I'm ready. You need time, not me. We can't go back and forth, waiting on each

❖

other's relationships to end. I've been grieving a real loss, crying genuine tears, and hurting from real pain."

It felt good to be honest, to say how I felt, if only for a minute.

"I can't help feeling the way I do about you and the things I've dreamed about with you," he said, "but I guess it's just not prudent to say them. This will only cause more pain. I share a lot of visual images as you, and certainly I know you love me and that this could be my biggest regret. I believe I'm just like you were when we met. You know you were in a shaky relationship when you met me, but you couldn't move because you were in it and had a responsibility until it was over, and I respected that a great deal."

I could've reminded him that he hadn't been in that relationship for that long and that he'd obviously met this woman since we'd been talking again, but what would've been the point?

"It's so hard to hold back what I have in my heart and visions," he wrote. "I wanted for us to have a nation together, to teach them the wisdom of Our Father. No doubt, they would be leaders of tomorrow."

"When did you stop wanting that? Why didn't you just come back to me?"

There was another long pause. Was he in as much pain as I was? Did he cry for me as I did for him?

Finally, I took a deep breath and typed the words that would signal good-bye. "I'm just glad to have been loved by you, even if it was for a brief time."

A moment's pause, and then it came:

"Nakupenda, Malaika."

"Nakupenda, Jaja.

❖

Track 17

Misplaced Love

Many times,
I sit and wonder why,
Why you left me, baby.

We were good,
So good together,
Don't understand how
You left me.

Misplaced love,
Dim decisions,
Reminiscence,
Supple touches,
Warm embraces,
Gentle kisses.
I don't care anymore,

Don't care anymore,
Just don't care anymore,
Why you left me.

Dreams
Of lives together,
You could throw away years.
You left me.

Promises.
A comfort to this fool.
Believed every word.
You left me.

Even after that, I tried to stay in contact with him. I would email him or send a text message to his phone almost daily, but I got no response from my Jaja. There were no more special emails meant only for me. Instead, he sent random emails every three to four months, containing a joke or a product recall that was sent to everyone on his contact list. Those made me so angry. They rubbed my face in the fact that I wasn't special to him anymore. And so I resisted. I would sign in online as soon as I had a free moment. Perhaps, I would hear that door squeak, signaling that one of my buddies had signed on. But I hoped in vain.

By that time, my finances had gotten really bad again. I fell behind on everything. The community service I was providing made me feel great, but it paid too little to live on. Antonio was still on the run from his child support case. I couldn't have counted on him for any financial support, anyway. I was back to making decisions on whether to pay rent and buy food, or pay the car insurance and maintenance, or utilities and toiletries. My car had no brake lights or

❖

insurance, so I couldn't be out after dark. I would have to press on the brakes half a block before a light or turning a corner, so no one would rear end me. Every day someone would flag me down to tell me my brake lights were out. I would pretend to be shocked and thank them graciously. I'd pull over, wait until they were out of sight, and then get back on the road again. I needed help, but I couldn't bring myself to ask for it.

Mom came to visit for the holidays and saw how bad our conditions were. She'd asked me to move "up North" before, but I'd always refused. I wanted to make a life for my kids and me on my own. But by then, I felt like I was good at nothing but failure. I was forced to admit defeat again. I had nowhere to go but to Mom's house. Something in my life needed to be a success.

A phone call from Naja finally convinced me to leave Florida and go "make some real money." I was emotionally spent, so it didn't take much convincing. I needed to go. I needed some relief.

When Felix found out that I was leaving, he tried to convince me to stay. He even hinted at helping me financially. His sudden interest in my well-being surprised me.

When we were together, I used to tell him that I was going to move away to make a better life for my kids and me. He'd smirk and say, "So, what's stopping you?" It hurt to hear him say that, but I pretended not to be affected.

So his new interest in our welfare was strange, all the more so since he and I hadn't seen each other in more than a year.

Felix was a man of few words, but he was talking a lot now and I was listening. He beat around the bush and brought up his immigration status again.

❖

Finally, he asked me to marry him. He was absolutely serious. I was shocked and did everything in my power not to smile. For once, I had the upper hand.

I reminded him I was still married to my daughter's father and Felix agreed to pay for my divorce. I told him that I'd already put in my two-week notice and he said that he would make it work. You know what I was thinking. Payback is a be-yatch!

Two weeks later, I packed up my life again and moved up yonder, to Virginia. No, Felix didn't offer to help me pack the truck. So I called on old faithful Brandon, Mr. Bi-Polar himself. He had my entire apartment on the truck in less than two hours.

That move in January 2004 just about undid me.

I knew my emotional state was fragile, but I had no idea how fragile. Heading north, I drove my rented U-Haul right into the worst snowstorm Virginia had seen in seven years. But that wasn't the worst of it.

Once I arrived in Virginia, I felt mentally paralyzed. I only spoke when I absolutely needed to. The decision to leave Florida extremely upset me. I had left all of my friends, my plans for the community center and given up my car. Once again, I'd had to give away all of the furniture I'd worked so hard to acquire because I had no means to store it. Now, I was back at home, living with Mom again, with no job, no money, and no direction. I didn't even own a winter coat. To say I had a bad case of the winter blues would be an understatement.

Even though I thought of Jaja daily, I tried to move on. By spring, I was working two jobs to catch up on my bills. My full-time job was working for another non-profit. I taught employability skills to

❖

men and women who received public assistance. I taught them how to fill out job applications, compose resumes, and make cold calls to potential employers. I talked to them about how to dress professionally and how to interview.

I thoroughly enjoyed the job because it enabled me to make a difference in people's lives. I helped men and woman gain the confidence and the skills necessary to convince employers to hire them. After attending my group sessions, many people who had never worked before were able to get jobs. Others returned to school to earn their high school equivalencies or college degrees. That was the kind of work I was meant to do; it was my passion.

My salary was more than it was in Orlando, but the higher cost of living ate up the difference. I wasn't making ends meet, not at all, so I took a second job.

It was at Ruby Tuesdays. I gave away my first few meals free because I couldn't keep the orders straight. One of the other servers, a guy named Michael, got me out of the weeds many times. He took my tables when I fell behind. Michael was cool and had a great sense of humor. He kept asking me out. The third time he offered, I took him up on it. He was twenty-four years old and had a roommate who also worked at the restaurant. I assumed they were college students like everyone else. (At 33, I was the oldest person working there. Even my manager was younger than me.)

One evening, I went over to Michael's apartment to watch Sunday Night Smack Down. I couldn't stand wrestling, but since everyone from the restaurant would go over I decided to check it out. When I got to his apartment, I found the room full of marijuana smoke. Everyone was sitting on the floor or

❖

holding up a wall because there was no furniture except for a couch. If you weren't one of the first four people there, you had plenty of floor space to choose from.

Later, I learned that the only passions Michael had, besides wrestling, were video games and rapping. One evening, I took him to see Bobby McFerrin in a free concert at the Kennedy Center. Michael told me that for the past five years he hadn't been anywhere but to work and back. That was also when I found out that being a server *was* his career. He wasn't a college student at all; he was a high school dropout.

That news was disconcerting enough. What really got me was when he told me his political affiliation. How in the world can a black man, making $9,000 a year and uneducated, have the nerve to be a Republican? We argued about that all the time. He would tell me that I didn't have any original thought. I don't know why people resort to insults when they disagree. I could have said a lot about his condition, but didn't. It just didn't seem like a fair fight.

That part-time job was harder than my full-time one. I was always exhausted and my body hurt from being on my feet all weekend. So I left the restaurant after working there a little over a year and got a job at the gym where I worked out. I sat behind the check-in desk the entire night, except at closing, when I had to wipe down the machines and clean the men's urinals.

For the next year I went back and forth between Virginia and Orlando, filing papers for the divorce that Felix was generous enough to pay for. It was nice to feel the Florida heat on my face again. I missed the palm trees, hanging out with my friends, and eating roti. Since Antonio was still nowhere to be

❖

found, I had to file on the grounds of abandonment. I put ads in newspapers, searched death records, motor vehicle, prison records, and unemployment records to find him, all to no avail.

Felix would greet me with a smile, a hug and a kiss when I got off the plane. He'd never greeted me that way before, even when we were good. He even bought me dinner. The last time Felix had taken me out was on our first date, five years earlier. Best of all, after ten years of separation from Antonio, I was finally getting a divorce.

I tried another attempt at dating. This time I went online. I didn't like going out by myself and since I didn't have any girlfriends in Virginia, online dating seemed like the next best option. It was fun at first. I had some great conversations. But I quickly learned that online dating was fast. People didn't take the time to get to know you at all. After two, maybe three, conversations, some guy I'd known only by his screen name would want to meet and often send explicit photos of his genitalia. I blocked a lot of users. It was worse than going to the club.

But it was fun to check my profile and see if anyone wanted to meet me. I received one wink from a gorgeous man. His username was "Intelligence." Finally! I immediately IM'd him back. We talked for about a month before he asked to meet. He had no problems with meeting me on my terms. He was a professional, said he liked to work out and was at the gym every day. So I met him one day after work for a glass of lemonade. He drove up in a beautiful white Lexus. That was nice. But when he stepped out of his car, I almost ran in the opposite direction. His feet were ashy and he had on sandals with thick black straps with Velcro closures, the same kind my nephew

❖

wore when he was three years old and slue-footed. And did he have the nerve to tell me he worked out? And how old was he? And whose picture did he use? At least I got a free glass of lemonade.

Sam was different. We talked online for two months before he asked to meet me. I met him at a pool hall. After a few drinks, he decided tell me the whole truth and nothing but the truth. Alcohol wasn't his liquid courage; it became his truth serum. I could look over him being white; I could look over him being shorter than me, but I had a time dealing with the fact that he was an ex-con who'd just been released from prison for selling drugs. Damn! Damn! Damn!

That was my last attempt at online dating. I deleted my profile. Actually, I was done trying to date at all.

D-day. September 11, 2005. I remember it as vividly as I did the pleasure dreams I used to have about Noel. I walked into the courthouse, passed through thirty minutes of security, and observed a moment of silence to commemorate the victims of 9/11. Then, at exactly 10:00 a.m., I joined sixteen other men and women in entering the judge's chambers. One by one, at the slamming of the gavel, we were pronounced divorced.

The moment wasn't as euphoric as I thought it would be, but my sense of joy got an extra lift from knowing that Felix was paying for the divorce. Felix picked me up at the courthouse and took me for a celebratory drink. A couple of hours later, I boarded a plane and headed home to Virginia. I was a little nervous because now I would have to let Felix know that I'd never intended to marry him.

❖

When I got off the plane, I found a message on my phone from him, telling me he knew that I used him. My cousin, Penny, had told him. The two of them had become prayer buddies after he found Jesus. I guess the information lay heavy on her heart and she felt she just had to tell him. Or maybe it was simply that she couldn't wait to steal my thunder. It was payback for telling Mom that Penny's husband had left her after Penny asked me not to.

When I got home, the first thing I did was go online to tell Noel of my new freedom. Somewhere deep, deep, deep in my gut, I thought this would make him as excited as I was. He'd always celebrated my joys before. To my surprise, I found an email from him sent two days earlier and addressed only to me.

Talk about butterflies in my stomach! I put my hand to my tummy to calm it as I read his words.

```
From:    Noel Wellington
Sent:    9 9 05
To:      Ayo
Subject: Nia Malaika Wellington

Greetings Ayo,

    I want you to meet my daughter,
Nia Malaika Wellington. Darling, you
have always inspired me and I really
hope my daughter will have a spirit
and personality as you do, hence the
name (Malaika).

Nakupenda,

Noel
```

❖

It took a few minutes for his words to sink in. I didn't understand what I'd just read. Then I realized that the love of my life had just attached a picture of the love of his life and their daughter.

Track 18

Eban

I'll conquer the world,
Just wait and watch my life unfurl.
My path is lit, future bright.
'Cause I snatched back like a thief in the night.
For years I struggled to find my worth.
Reached out for it, attempting to unearth,
But your words were too heavy,
For me to carry.
And I removed myself from life,
And hid from constant strife.
Light faded; and I grew wary of my ability.
It left me weak.
I allowed you took my will and every piece of my
sanity.
Opened my heart to you,

And was forced to choose
Between you and my happiness.
I take full responsibility for what I allowed to be.
It is up to me,
To end this cycle
So go away and never return,
Because I am ending this to have the life I yearn.

Two and a half years passed. One day, soon after I
kicked Brandon out, the telephone rang. It was Noel. I
had long ago stopped thinking of him as my guardian
angel and praying that God would make him mine.
Nevertheless, the sound of Noel's voice filled me with
joy. It resonated like the most beautiful love song I'd
ever heard.

We caught up on old times and discovered that
the last couple of years had been wearisome for us
both. He and his daughter's mother, Mona, had called
it quits and he was raising their child alone. I
pretended to be happy and have my life together,
when in fact every tomorrow was a scary thought. I'd
always been good at faking my pain.

One of the reasons Noel and I didn't have a real
relationship was because we lived so far apart. He
always had an issue with me living in the States and
he in Jamaica. He said he didn't think I could handle
life in Jamaica and that he had no intentions of ever
moving to the States. I worked hard for almost four
years to get him to change his mind, but it wasn't
enough. He grew tired of our Internet affair and
moved on to live his life with his new love.

We talked every week for the next four months.
For the first time he made comments about us being
together for real and soon. When he first mentioned it
I wasn't happy about it because he'd broken my heart

❖

and it was finally healed. I wasn't ready to give him access to old wounds again.

How dare he after all this time come back in my life like that, especially when he knew how much l loved him, when he knew that I was sitting by my phone and in front of my computer, waiting for him to be mine. Especially after he knew how much I hurt when I learned that he was a new father via an email when I hadn't spoken to him in years. I was reminded of the times I would give a man my heart but it wasn't enough to keep him. After they'd realize that a pretty smile and big ass isn't all it's cracked up to be, they would try to get me back. It brought back memories of not feeling good enough, of feeling like a last option. I was angry with him for making me feel that way.

But eventually I allowed myself to be vulnerable and let him in again. We began making plans to see each other soon. I decided to tell him everything that I'd gone through. I would no longer hide from my situation. I had to confess that I'd given up on my happiness and settled on the familiar, and that by doing so I'd messed up again. It was a gamble. Suppose he was so disappointed in me that he turned away? I was running a risk, but it was a risk I had to take.

"Did you complete your book?" he asked.

"No."

I was embarrassed. I knew what was coming next.

"Ayo, you are full of great ideas, but you don't complete any of them."

"You're right. Now say something nice about me."

We both laughed.

❖

"Well, that's not all," I finally said. "I've managed to get myself in another bind." I hesitated. How could I tell him? I finally had a real chance with him and I was about to lose it. For the next thirty minutes, I beat around the bush and gave not-so-subtle hints.

Finally, he asked, "Are you pregnant?"

I wasn't ready to tell him, but I had to.

"Seven months," I said.

"That's heavy."

"I know."

"I'm not okay with this."

I pretended not to hear him. I knew I'd just lost him again. I continued the conversation as if nothing were wrong.

"You're only the fourth person I've told. My daughter knows, the doctor knows, and the lady who performed the ultrasound knows."

"What about the father?"

"I told him in an email when I first found out. He hasn't contacted me since. I don't know where he is."

I told him a little about Brandon and what I'd been through with him. I said I hadn't told anyone else because I was so full of negativity that I couldn't bear to hear anymore. So I chose to face it alone.

"I will tell you the truth out of love, Ayo. You know that don't you?"

"Yes."

He went on to express his disappointment and I let him, just as I allowed everyone else to do in my life. When he was done, I hung up, gently, quietly. I felt numb, like a zombie, but that was good, because it let me function for the rest of the day.

❖

It surprised me at first that I didn't cry. I didn't even have the impulse to cry. If anything, I felt cold inside, cold and dead.

Late that evening, I made tea and tried to meditate – tried being the key word. Whenever I tried to sink into myself, I found that cold spot inside me, the part that was frozen with grief. I thought about it.

Was it grief or anger? Or a mixture of both?

I touched my belly. How could the baby live with such cold? I didn't want these terrible feelings to be transmitted to my child. This little one deserved better. I couldn't give him material wealth, but I could strive for spiritual health.

Without giving myself a chance to hesitate, I went to the telephone and placed a call. I didn't really expect to find him at home – he was usually out that time of night – but he answered.

"Ayo," he said. "Are you all right?"

He was obviously surprised. He also sounded worried, as if he cared, really cared about what happened to me. Hours earlier, my heart would've leapt for joy at his tone of concern. But that was the old Ayo. The new one had a very different set of turn-ons.

"No," I said. "I'm not all right. And I will tell you why."

My voice was deathly calm. I didn't even recognize it as my own. But it was me, the real me, the strong me who'd finally found her voice because she had nothing left to lose.

"Ayo?"

He actually sounded scared. Well, he had good reason to be.

"Earlier today, you said you were going to tell me the truth out of love. Well, ever since then, I've been wondering. Love for whom? You don't love anybody but your own damn self. You sure as hell don't love me. You just feel some sort of twisted obligation to me. Well, don't. I don't want you. Why would I? You're the most piss poor excuse for a man I have *ever* known."

I hadn't planned on saying that, but the moment the words left my mouth, I realized they were true. I realized something else, too, that the coldness inside me was warming up, that the frozen anger was not only thawing, it was heating up.

He tried to say something and I cut him off.

"Wait one goddamned minute, you self-righteous asshole. Who the hell do you think you're talking to? Don't even fix your lips to say another word to me, 'cause I ain't trying to hear it.

"I admit I was stupid. It took me this long to see you for what you are. To realize that you try to make yourself look good by making me look bad. Well, save that shit for the next dumb ass. You can keep your twisted kind of love for the next jackass."

"Calm down, Ayo. I will call you tomor––"

"No. Don't. I am so tired of your ass coming in and out of my life. But I let it happen. I sure did. I forgave your lying ass at every single turn."

"I never lied to you."

"The hell you didn't. You have lied and cheated from the very beginning. Back when we first met, you knew you were leaving the country and never intended to come back. Did you tell me? No? Well, that was a lie. When I visited you in Jamaica, you knew you had a girlfriend. Did you tell me? No? That was a lie, too. In both cases, you didn't say a damn thing until you absolutely had to. You cheated on me with her, and on her with me. But did I criticize you?

❖

Hell, no. I kept on loving your ass – but that's not the worst of it.

"You didn't contact me for a year. Fine. But when you did, it was to email me a picture of your love child and her mother. What did I do? I still loved you. God help me, I still loved you."

By now, the tears were rolling down my face and my hands were trembling. But my voice, it was sure. It was steady. It was like a hammer and I used it to land me some blows.

"So now, I will tell *you* the truth out of love. You're the most callous and calculating sonofabitch I have ever dealt with. You knew my pain and you played on it. Every time you pretended to help me, you were doing it because it made you feel a little more superior. Well, you're not superior. You're a mothafucking con artist!"

"Ayo––"

"And I used to think you were an angel sent by God." I paused, struck by a new thought. "Maybe you were. Maybe God wanted me to see just how slick a liar and cheater a false angel could be. You and your spirituality! All that time I spent looking up to you. What was I thinking?"

"You have no right––"

"Go to hell. Do you hear me Noel? Stay the fuck out of my life and go to hell."

I hung up and sat for a moment. The inner coldness was gone and so was the baking anger. There was grief, but not for him. If anything, it was grief for the dreams – the *fantasies* – I'd built around him.

I called Regina and told her what had happened. I also described how I'd spent the last few months journaling my life, hoping to shake these monkeys off my back. After I finished, she didn't say

❖

anything. That was odd. Regina always had something to say, whether I wanted to hear it or not.

"Regina?"

"I'm here."

"No 'I told you so,' or, 'It's about time?'"

"Not this time. I'm proud of you, my little *nina tonta*."

She had just called me a naive little girl. "I understand Spanish, Regina."

"Oh, yeah."

We laughed.

"I guess I was tired of his shigidy," I said.

"And how do you feel now?"

I paused. Only one word came to mind: "Free."

After talking to Regina, I emailed Brandon to let him know that our son's due date was May 7th. He had some not so nice words to say. He's added me to the long list of people who have let him down. I wanted to tell him to go build his own *eban* but he's not ready.

Three months have passed since Noel learned I was pregnant. It's also been three months since I've spoken to him and I could care less.

Brandon failed to contact me but his mother has. She said he was in a car accident and smashed up his knee. She also claims she doesn't know his whereabouts.

Felix and Dorthea reconciled. Felix emailed me a while back saying that he and Dorthea are back together. His battle to be a good Christian husband battles his desires of the flesh. They bought a new house in Winter Park, Florida.

Things are looking up for me as well. I had my six-month review at my job yesterday and not only got an unexpected raise, but was also offered a

❖

promotion. When I got home today, I got a letter from child support. Antonio will pay $237 a month. It's not nearly enough for taking care of Kaiya, but it's something. I'm just glad he's finally going to help support Kaiya. It'll pay for her braces, if nothing else.

When I was thirty-eight weeks pregnant, I started to show. I still hadn't told anyone about my pregnancy and I didn't have anything for the baby either. When Asha, a co-worker, noticed my baby bump and realized I was dealing with it alone, she made sure I had everything a newborn baby would need. She took me shopping, found donated items and helped me find a great pediatrician. Anagha, another co-worker, found out I was pregnant the day before I went into labor and dropped everything to be by my side.

Kaiya and Asha stayed with me during my thirty hours of labor, helping me to breathe and stay calm. Anagha held my hand during my Caesarean. My son, Omar Jamal, was born on May 7th at 1:48 a.m., weighing 6 lb. 10 oz. When the nurse put him in my arms I felt a sense of overwhelming love and well-being.

Coincidentally, May 7th is also Mom's birthday. Fresh from the operating room I called her to send her best wishes and to mention that she had a new grandbaby. She was stunned, of course, and asked why I hadn't told her about my pregnancy. I breezed over it and changed the subject. Mom didn't need an explanation. She new the pregnancy was emotional and at the end of that phone call I knew that she would be there for us. She was clearly hurt, but put her feelings aside and concentrated on the baby and me.

❖

Back home from the hospital, I found a box of baby items with a card attached. "If you need anything don't hesitate to ask, Rex and Trixie." Rex and Trixie are my next-door neighbors. They'd seen me out doing yard work for the past few months and respectfully said nothing about my growing belly. They just waved and kept going as good neighbors do. Periodically, they now leave food and bags of goodies at the front door.

It took my writing to show me that I am talented and deserved to follow my dreams and I applied to film school.

It took my son's birth to show me that when it comes to receiving love I'm not limited to the branches of our family tree. I can look further to get what I need. Regina and Lei have been great sisters to me; Anagha, and Asha are great cousins; Rex and Trixie make a great aunt and uncle; and, Alfonza and Savannah are two of the best emotionally supportive parental figures one could ever ask for.

❖

Track 19

My Souls Reflection

When I looked in the mirror,
I didn't recognize the stare.
All I saw were two big, brown eyes
Staring back at me.
Those eyes were full of pain beyond despair
When I smiled to comfort her,
There was no response.
I needed to feel good again,
So I wrote down my thoughts.
I understand my life through the words I write.
It's clear.
I let others dictate my life.
I have a story that needs to be told,
Turn the pages and watch it unfold.
I hold the pen that dictates my future,

It closes my wounds like the surgeon's suture.
Today I start the first chapter of the rest of my life.
I have the power to make it right.

Sonia Matthews spent years battling the residual effects of domestic violence. Now, she helps victims become empowered.

Proceeds from the sale of *When Life Becomes A Love Story* will go toward educational scholarships for individuals who struggle with self-sufficiency.

Sonia believes through education comes empowerment, the ability to leave potentially life-threatening situations, and the ability to walk through any open door.

soniamatthews.com

Read and Empower Lives!

Printed in the United States
220035BV00001B/4/P

9 780981 587400